# *be your own*
# Moon Astrologer

# *be your own* Moon Astrologer

## Transform your life using the Moon's signs and cycles

Heather Roan Robbins

CICO BOOKS
LONDON NEWYORK

This edition published in 2019 by CICO Books
An imprint of Ryland Peters & Small Ltd
20–21 Jockey's Fields, London WC1R 4BW
341 E 116th St, New York NY 10029

www.rylandpeters.com

10 9 8 7 6 5

First published in 2015 under the title *Moon Wisdom*



A CIP catalog record for this book is available from the Library of Congress and the British Library.

ISBN: 978 1 78249 701 1

Printed in China

**Editor:** Marion Paull
**Illustrator:** Sarah Perkins

**Commissioning editor:** Kristine Pidkameny
**In-house editor:** Carmel Edmonds
**In-house designer:** Eliana Holder
**Art director:** Sally Powell
**Production controller:** Mai-Ling Collyer
**Publishing manager:** Penny Craig
**Publisher:** Cindy Richards

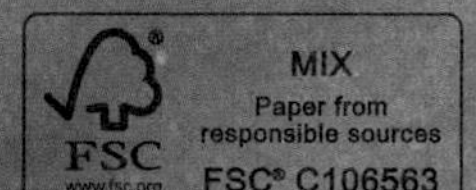


# Contents

# Introduction

Why have a disaster (dis=against, aster=the stars) when we can constellate instead (con=with, stella=stars)? It's my personal belief that we're not influenced by the planets but that the planets are influenced by the same universal patterns that influence us. My metaphor is that if you see horns above the fence you might not want to put your foot underneath it–the horns won't hurt your foot, but whatever moves the horns moves the hooves, and the horns (and planets) are easier to see. Use astrology to make your life easier and to explore your connection with the breath of the world and the cycles of the stars.

Here we look at astrology in two different dimensions. First we look at you, how you encapsulate the astrology of the moment of your birth (Part I: Your Moon Sign), what this implies about your personal nature, and how to inhabit that nature most comfortably. Then we look at the astrology of the moment (Part II: Navigate Your Day With the Moon), the astrological energetic weather conditions created by the signs and patterns of the planets as they are right now, and how best to engage those patterns for a full and happy life.

## What the Moon brings to the table

The Moon sets the tone of the day. As it shines through a sign, it colors our emotional milieu and lends us the gifts and strengths of that sign. The fastest of the celestial bodies we watch in astrology, it circles the Earth and moves through the whole zodiac in approximately 28 days, changing sign every two and a third days.

When you know where the Moon is on any given day, you get a snapshot of the general attitude and mood of the day, with clues about how to deal with people, how to navigate the subway in relative safety, and what to expect from your loved ones.

You may not always have a choice about when to tackle a challenge, but you can always choose your response. If you work against the sign of the Moon on any given day, it may make life harder, but it can be done with a little extra attention. For example, the extroverted Leo Moon brings an expansive, sociable, dramatic mood. If your taxes are due tomorrow but the Moon is in Leo and a party beckons, it may not be easy to keep your nose to the grindstone. Bribe yourself with the promise of a little Leonine indulgence or social outlet along the way.

Likewise, it might be prudent to avoid going to court with a jealous ex just as the Moon enters brooding and suspicious Scorpio, but if you have to, you can go in prepared with shields up, willpower on, and ready not to take the bait for a fight. If you had a choice, life would be so much more comfortable if you did your taxes under a careful, introspective Virgo Moon and scheduled your divorce-court date under a freedom-loving, forgiving Sagittarius Moon.

These basic astrological guidelines apply to anybody's chart, but the Moon will affect each one of us differently as it reacts with our own natal chart. Just as a farmer with parched fields will respond to a report of rain differently from a lover about to set up a picnic, how we respond to the Moon in Aries versus the Moon in Cancer depends upon our own chart and situation. So it helps to take notes about our personal responses to the cycles of the Moon. An interesting benefit accrues with this work when you notice how moods change in response to the Moon's cycles. You feel the same, but become less identified by, and attached to, your personal mood, and therefore mediate your feelings more comfortably.

When you were born, you imprinted the astrological pattern of that birth moment and live out that pattern, with a lot of choice about how, for the rest of your life. Most people know their Sun sign. The Sun spends a month in each sign at more or less the same time every year and gives us the skeletal underpinnings for the rest of the chart, but it only tells us part of the picture. The rest of the chart does that.

What sign the Moon shines through at the moment you were born describes the deep inner river of your emotions—what motivates you, how you express your feelings, and how you nurture and need nurturing. It records the history of your female lineage and emotional training, it describes your daily habits, such as how you cook or train your dog, all the little things that we take for granted but may not make sense to others.

The Moon sign also speaks of a primary emotional need that we bring into this life, and through which the universe seems to trick us into our toughest work. But if we come to know and own this primary need, this prime directive, we can take charge of our accomplishments in a healthy and proactive way.

## How to use this book

Part I describes how to cultivate the potential of your Moon sign. Go to www.astro.com for a free astrological chart (see page 154 for more ideas) to find out where the Moon was at the moment you were born. Read that Moon sign, and investigate how to engage your Moon sign more comfortably. If you don't know the minute you were born and the Moon changes sign that day, read both signs and see if one fits more clearly than the other.

Look up the important people in your life—spouse, parents, children, coworkers, or boss—read their Moon-sign attributes, and use those clues to relate more easily with them.

Part II describes the astrological weather, the mood of the day under that Moon sign. Go online or to your astrological calendar (see page 152) to find out where the Moon is today.

Read the section for the Moon and see how it fits your personal experience. Notice the strengths of each Moon sign, what to watch out for, how to nurture your romance under that sign. Under each Moon you will also find a line about gardening that applies both to the garden around your house and, metaphorically, to the garden of projects and ideas you might like to grow.

Keep a journal about your own reaction to each Moon. How do you feel, what do you want to do or not want to do? Notice which Moon days are comfortable for you and which are challenging, and begin to make plans that correlate. If you find you are weepy but creative under a Pisces Moon, stay home and paint. If you're charming and socially aware, plan to interact.

Once you have a feel for the Moon's effect through the signs, venture into Part III where we layer in the qualities of the Moon's phases to help you work with the soul's tides and time your efforts to your best advantage. Fine tune this work by looking at the Moon's aspects, its relationship to the other planets in our solar system, in both the birth chart and through daily planning.

# Part I
# Your Moon Sign

Explore the imprint of the sign and phase of the Moon on your birth moment and on the birth moments of those close to you. This will give you greater self-awareness and help you understand, and deal with more effectively, loved ones, friends, and colleagues.

# The map of your life

At our first breath of life, we internalize the patterns of the moment as a blueprint or map for our personality this lifetime. We live out that map, with a lot of choice over how, for the rest of our life. Whether we choose to be born at a moment that symbolically resonates with our soul work or whether we are affected by the universal patterns present at the moment of our birth, no one really knows. Astrologers see a synchronicity, a correlation between the cycles of the planets of our solar system and the emotional map of our life.

The Sun takes a month in each sign and describes the basic skeleton or structure of our personality. Most of us know the answer to the question, "What sign are you?" The Moon takes just two and a half days in each sign and describes our inner emotional nature underneath that structure.

♈ ♉ ♊ ♋ ♌ ♍

Think of this layering as if you had cut into a blood orange. This fruit may look like an orange on the outside, but within you find rich, red pulp. If you dissect the personality of someone born with the Sun in Aries and Moon in Cancer, that person may look and act like an impulsive Aries on the outside, but feel like a sensitive, thoughtful Cancer Moon on the inside, and this layering makes each one of us subtler and more interesting.

Where the Moon was situated when we were born reflects our deepest emotions, what makes us feel at home, and propensities that become ingrained in childhood. It describes daily habits that we take for granted but seem odd to others. This section gives us clues to understanding and working with our own temperament and those of the people around us.

♎ ♏ ♐ ♑ ♒ ♓

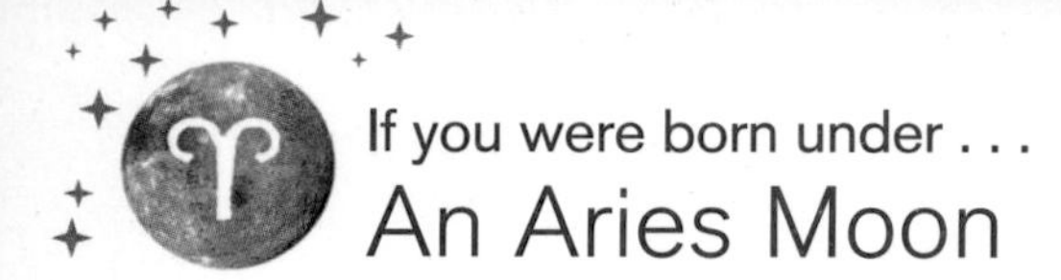

If you were born under . . .

# An Aries Moon

You have fire at your core. Your heart is brave and generous and you are independent, outspoken, and inherently anti-authoritarian. You are also self-directed and can be brusque, even appear rude if distracted or on task, but underneath may feel warm-hearted and protective.

## Challenges

Like a spring thunderstorm, your temper probably spikes quickly and disappears. After you express displeasure, you may feel refreshed and wonder why everybody else is still upset. You tend to the "ready, fire, aim" mentality and can react before thinking it through and so miss long-term ramifications. You can also be contrary to the point of shooting yourself in the foot. Boredom and repetition can make you careless. Develop impulse control and a little patient tolerance of slower people around you. Think about what you really want. You need to move out of reaction and into leadership to turn your challenges into gifts.

## Primary emotional need

The soul says, "I need to do this myself. I need to explore new territory. I need to do it my way." You can have an underlying unconscious belief that if your need is deferred, it will not be met. You may assume that it's safer to do it yourself and forget to include others in decision-making processes. As you evolve, you can move away from contention and into direction, from complex reaction to simple but dynamic creation. As you age, you'll want to stay author of your own life for as long as possible.

## Dealing with those born under an Aries Moon

Don't make them wait. Say what you mean and mean what you say. Those born under an Aries Moon like strength. You don't have to agree with them, just respect their opinions. Aries Moon people are comfortable with your independence as long as they are neither waiting nor worried. Waiting can turn their minds to emergencies, and they can become controlling and directive when anxious, so stay in touch and give reassurance. Tempers can spike quickly. If you see that an Aries Moon person is winding up, back off. Once their defenses are up, they can be a real challenge to deal with.

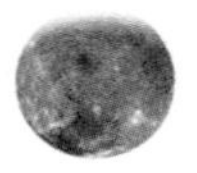

**At work** Aries Moon people are self-directed, but clear deadlines help them to stay focused and on track. Consensus is not their idea of a good time. Establish common goals, clarify expectations, and let them find their own way there. They can be brusque, appear rushed, and want to give an order just once. Their mood is contagious, whether an inspiring enthusiasm or bitter rebellion, so invest in a mutually useful understanding. Don't brag, just do; let them feel your competence.

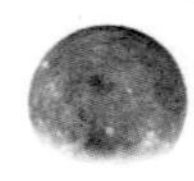

**In romance** When they were growing up, many people born under an Aries Moon were told, "Don't be so intense." Never make that mistake. Find a way to love their bright fire. Give them room for independence but feel free to negotiate for your own needs. It's good to let them see you have a full and independent life away from them, but do not play games. Run with the passionate moments and enjoy a sense of adventure and spontaneity together. They love new experiences, new territory, but they don't pick up new routines easily. If you need something, use "I" statements and spell it out; they may not always understand subtle hints.

**In the family** A little secure routine is good for Aries Moon children, but a lot will make them rebellious. Help them to develop a clear and responsible way to express their temper. Encourage a healthy sense of humor and true independent thinking so they're not manipulated by a dare. Choice and self-direction are lifeblood to them; reward them with free time or spontaneous adventure.

Aries Moon parents can often give family members a hard time, but they will stand up fiercely for their family against outsiders. Let them know you hear them, even if you disagree; otherwise arguments will escalate. Rather than resist their willfulness, be curious about them and they'll be curious about you.

As Aries Moon relatives age, give them freedom and choice over protection wherever possible. The song "I Did It My Way" would be a suitable choice for their funeral.

# Gifts of an Aries Moon

**Initiative:** You are often the first one on the dance floor or the first to the top of the mountain.

**Energy:** You operate with enthusiasm and charisma when you're emotionally engaged.

**Resilience:** You are good in an emergency and can multitask under stress.

**Spontaneity:** You expect, even enjoy, the unexpected, and are usually up for adventure.

**Strength:** You can handle life events that would crush others and can loan strength to support others when needed. But just because you're strong enough to handle a tough situation doesn't mean you need to stay there. Ask if it's really for the highest good of all involved, you included, to hang in there.

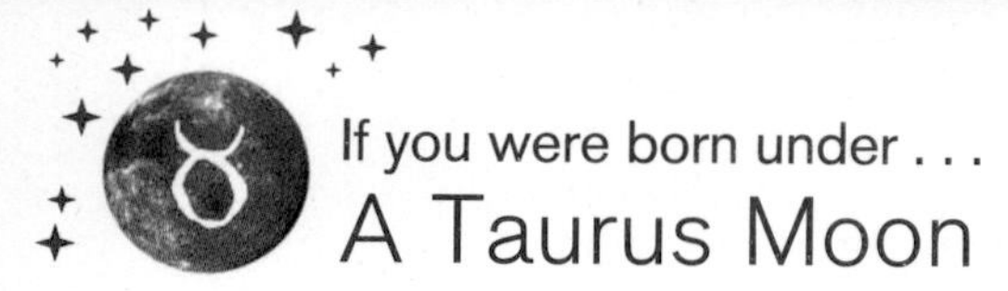

If you were born under . . .

# A Taurus Moon

You have a warm, steady, enduring, pragmatically creative nature. You may have a gift with the material world, your garden, your lovemaking, or your portfolio. You hate to be rushed, and are more comfortable working and learning at your own steady pace, but you like to see projects through–once you've got it, you've got it. You put down roots and like a lush and cozy environment. You also root in relationships; once you know people are trustworthy and do what they say they're going to do, you can bond deeply to friend or partner. It doesn't hurt if they are luscious, too; you do love beauty.

## Challenges

Once your heels dig in and your chin juts out, the opposition can just forget it. Sometimes your strength becomes stubbornness, "won't" power versus "will" power. Your challenge is to be both stable and flexible. Although you can be generous, you can be haunted by possessiveness and don't like to share. You are neither fond of someone looking at your mate nor stealing a pickle off your plate. You can overindulge in cashmere, sex, or chocolate cake. Your collections and memorabilia can become clutter unless you learn to edit your physical surroundings.

## Primary emotional need

You may have come into this life asking for stability but forgot to ask for good stability. Prisons can be stable. So be specific. Work to create a sustainable ecology out of your life, so you give back what you put into it and live a life with bread and roses.

Like a tree reaching into fertile soil, you need to grow roots in a good career, relationship, and place that feeds you. Be willing to leave what is only okay to search for something that will really help you bear fruit.

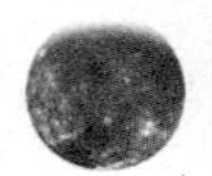

## Dealing with those born under a Taurus Moon

To help Taurus Moon people feel at home, make them comfortable, offer them some yummy food, and do not surprise them. They are not fond of change that they did not initiate, so don't alter plans at the last minute. It would be better to promise less and pleasantly surprise them with more, than not to come through on an agreement. Don't try to rush them or push them into anything; instead, invite and seduce, share your vision, help them to see both the practical outcomes and the steps needed to get there. Appreciate them just as they are, because although they may grow and evolve, they rarely change dramatically.

At work Taurus Moons thrive in a secure work environment and in jobs that have clear and steady expectations, putting their creative determination, sociable collaboration, and ability to follow through to good use. They can work steadily until the job is done; just don't spring sudden deadlines on them. Collaboration and bonuses inspire them, stress does not.

Taurus Moon bosses will want to know they are getting their money's worth out of their workers. They may be risk-averse but can nurture talent.

In romance Feed the senses of Taurus Moons, give them beautiful things, and enjoy experiencing the world with them, whether walking through the woods (bring a delicious picnic) or sharing a night on the town. Express affection through touch and

sensuality. Respect their need for your loyalty, and honor their loyalty to you. Set healthy financial boundaries, because they can spend money, yours included, but can also stick within a friendly budget once it's well defined.

**In the family** Taurus Moon children need security and art supplies. Help them to feel safe as they explore possibilities and listen to their fruitful creative nature. They need touch and snuggling, possibly a security blanket, the routine of a story and a hug goodnight.

Parents born under a Taurus Moon hate surprises being sprung upon them. They prefer family rituals and may be unusually strict about curfews. Help them to develop new family habits that work as the family grows.

Seniors need to feel plans are well in place for their safety and comfort.

# Gifts of a Taurus Moon

**Steadiness:** You can be the rock of Gibraltar, a pillar of strength and stability for others.

**Abundance:** Like a fruit tree, once you feel stable and rooted, you can produce abundance and comfort for yourself and others. Your kitchen is usually well-stocked, although you may appreciate a hearty, well-cooked meal more than fine delicacies.

**Cuddliness:** You can be a great hugger, a good lover, and often have a beautiful voice.

**Good taste:** You create beauty in your surroundings and have a natural eye for worthy collectibles.

**Good business sense:** You have a good sense of financial worth and natural instincts to grow resources.

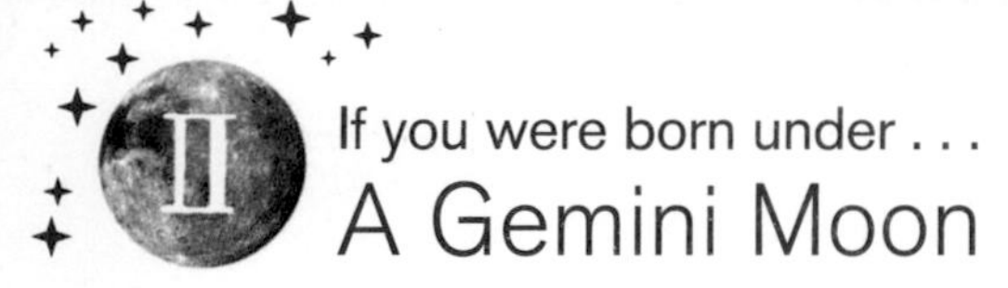

# If you were born under . . . A Gemini Moon

✦ You are mentally quick and can talk to just about anybody at any time. You're a born networker and can get along with disparate people, putting them at ease with gracious conversation. If you found a thief in your home, you might strike up a conversation so you could get out safely and give a good description to the police later.

## Challenges

Your mercurial mind can multitask and cross-reference with ease, but you get bored easily, and when you get bored, you make mistakes. Since it's easy for you to talk, and you talk even more when you're nervous, you can dominate a conversation. You're good at teasing secrets out of people, but not so good at keeping those secrets unless you are specifically asked to do so; all information is fodder for your wonderful stories. Even though you're a natural extrovert, you can get anxious because you can be so nervy and aware and need time alone to retract your antennae. Your versatility can be taken for granted, and you may be asked to adapt when it's your turn to have your needs met. Make sure you are as aware of your own as you are of others' needs. Learn to calm your busy nervous system, keep your heart connected to your head, and quietly deepen your mind.

## Primary emotional need

You came into this life to learn to communicate under any circumstance and to reach across the aisle and reconcile opposites. As a child, you may have had to adapt to very

different strong personalities around you, to understand relatives or neighbors who didn't understand each other. This promoted your intelligence and versatile capacity to connect, as well as an aversion for arguments. You need to know your beloveds care as much about your story as you do about theirs.

## Dealing with those born under a Gemini Moon

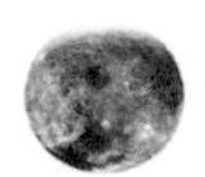

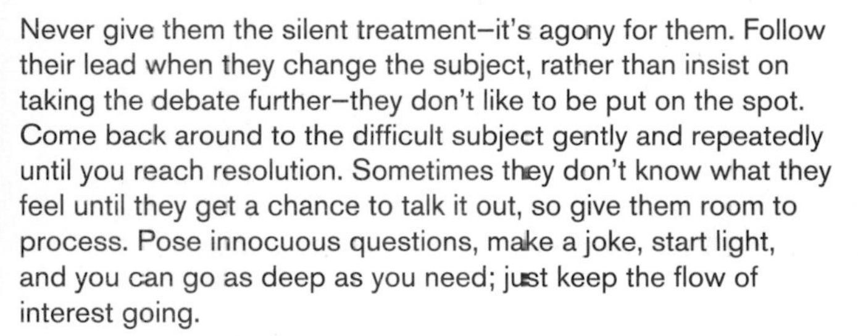

Never give them the silent treatment–it's agony for them. Follow their lead when they change the subject, rather than insist on taking the debate further–they don't like to be put on the spot. Come back around to the difficult subject gently and repeatedly until you reach resolution. Sometimes they don't know what they feel until they get a chance to talk it out, so give them room to process. Pose innocuous questions, make a joke, start light, and you can go as deep as you need; just keep the flow of interest going.

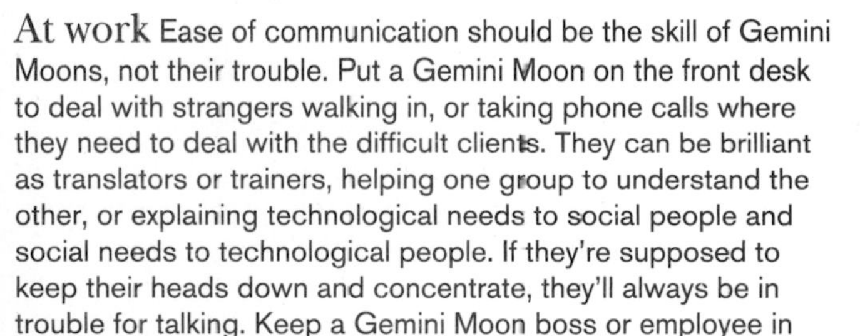

**At work** Ease of communication should be the skill of Gemini Moons, not their trouble. Put a Gemini Moon on the front desk to deal with strangers walking in, or taking phone calls where they need to deal with the difficult clients. They can be brilliant as translators or trainers, helping one group to understand the other, or explaining technological needs to social people and social needs to technological people. If they're supposed to keep their heads down and concentrate, they'll always be in trouble for talking. Keep a Gemini Moon boss or employee in the loop with constant updates.

**In romance** They love poetry, so let romance pour into your words. Text and e-mail throughout the day, share all the details at night. Don't give them a hard time if they need a moment

alone after a busy day; they'll soon be back refreshed. It isn't productive to be jealous about their gentle verbal flirtations or their need to stay connected to a wide circle of friends; they need to talk, not touch. They can honestly love more than one person, but are usually loyal once they make a commitment. Just don't assume that commitment has been made until they officially declare it.

**In the family** Gemini Moon children may have trouble sitting still for lessons at school. Work with them in short chunks with activity breaks between and they learn quickly. Take them on neighborhood adventures and help them to discern when it's safe to talk to strangers and when to keep to themselves.

Gemini Moon relatives may forget to ask your story and just assume that you'll jump in the conversation when you're ready, just like they do.

Older Gemini Moons need connection built into their daily lives and may require help to track details even when their minds are sharp.

# Gifts of a Gemini Moon

**Verbal ability:** You can easily imitate accents, pick up languages, and figure out the metaphor that will get the point across. You're a natural at social media and can think and speak in short sound bites.

**Sociability:** You can make friends easily, but may not let many truly close to your heart. Your nervous system vibrates and responds to everyone in the room.

**Adaptability:** Your fast, curious mind can synthesize and scintillate. You can adapt easily to respond to your environment.

**Being a natural translator:** You can find some point in common with just about anyone you meet, so you can help reach across cultural or social divides.

**Ability to deepen conversation:** When you want to, you are excellent at drawing people out and can use these interviewing and counseling skills widely.

If you were born under . . .

# A Cancer Moon

Your emotions and inspiration can run as deep as the ocean and be as complex and sensitive as life in a tidal pool. Since you pick up so much from others, you know what your community needs, but occasionally you prefer to spend time alone safely in your own shell. Intimacy is something you both crave and can be daunted by. Familiarity, people you can truly count on, a safe home sanctuary—all these mean the world to you and give you the security you need to express your natural leadership.

## Challenges

Your mood affects the people around you. You can be as cranky as a crab on the outside while you guard tender feelings inside and then wonder why people are so uncongenial in response. You hate feeling judged, which makes it uncomfortable for you to be out and about at times, or to put your work on public view. Your shell can lose its porousness, so you become isolated in your safe haven. It can be a challenge for you to ask directly for what you want; the more something matters to you, the more likely you are to become passive aggressive or withdraw. Find a comfortable way to be assertive and safely share your essential self.

## Primary emotional need

You came into this life to understand some primal truth about the nature of home, homeland, and family. You may have been born into a family where nurturing and security were not something you could take for granted, or may have come with strings attached, so real safety and familiarity are dear to you.

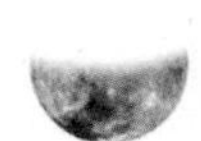

## Dealing with those born under a Cancer Moon

Take time to get to know Cancer Moon people and establish a personal relationship. They appreciate familiar places and faces, often returning to the same vacation spot and visiting the same stores. They like to know the grocer, the poet at the coffee shop, the people at the pub, the mailman. Those daily conversations help them to stay grounded and connected. They usually work quietly, behind the scenes, often in positions of responsibility, but if they have to work publicly, it will be in a low-key manner that makes their job look easy. In any case, they dearly need to be appreciated for their contributions.

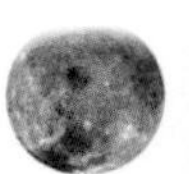

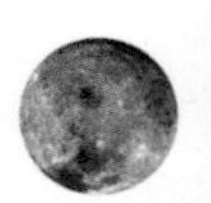

**At work** Abstract ideas alone are not enough for Cancer Moons, but they can run with big ideas and hard-core business if they can make a personal connection in the process. Cancer Moons can be self-conscious–focus on their accomplishments and not their performance and their performance improves.

Keep Cancer Moon bosses in the loop. If they feel you have their department's best interests in mind, they'll watch out for you. You can respectfully challenge their ideas with ease, but disrespect them personally and their claws come out.

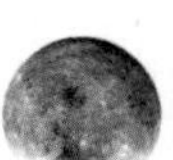

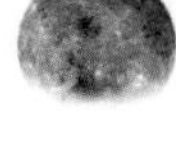

**In romance** Love them unabashedly. Whether or not they love you back, they will always respect you for caring. They need extra nurturing from their partner and tend to want to take care of their beloveds. While that's lovely, it's important to treat them as lovers and equals first. They need to grow into a family with you and become familiar with your quirks. Don't assume you know what makes them happy; get to know their aesthetics and priorities, then weave theirs together with yours. No matter how charismatic and outgoing they are otherwise, a corner of their soul will always need reassurance.

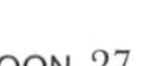

**In the family** As children, Cancer Moons need to spend time in their own world, safe from emotional dramatics. They may work to develop a persona or skill to be appreciated.

Cancer Moon parents are sometimes overprotective. If they are hurt, they tend to withdraw and leave you to make the next overture.

Older Cancer Moons want to stay in their own home for as long as possible. Ensure access to the few familiar foods they love and help them to distill their stories and memories.

# Gifts of a Cancer Moon

**Community building:** You help others to feel at home and so can weave connections within your community. If you ran a bar, the whole town would gather there.

**Heart inspiration:** You have an artist's soul, whatever your work, and aren't interested in making artistic compromises. Your work has to come from your inner source.

**Nurturing:** You can mother children, friends, a business, or a culture. A cup of tea at your kitchen table can do wonders for the soul.

**Intuition:** You can be a psychic sponge, so honor your hunches and check your facts.

**Protectiveness:** You can be as protective as a grizzly bear of your family, business, or posse.

**Nesting:** Like a crab that carries its home on its back, you need a home base. Having a sanctuary to return to helps you to go out and do what needs to be done.

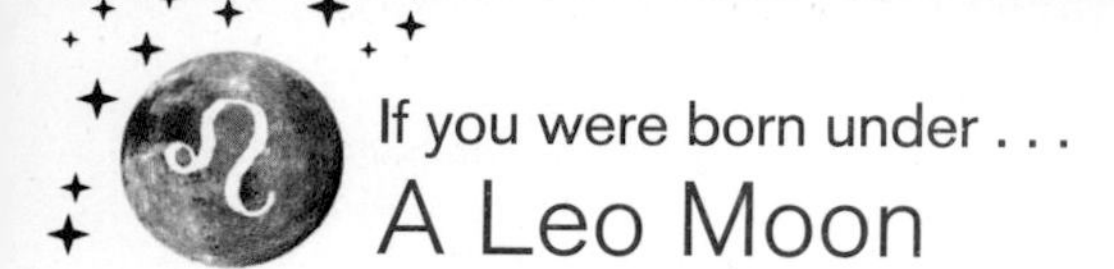

If you were born under . . .

# A Leo Moon

- You light up the room and can be the hearth fire that draws us all together. People thrive on your appreciation, when they are the center of your focus. You help anyone to feel that he/she is the only person on Earth. You like life to be exciting and are naturally good in dramatic situations, but you can stimulate your own drama if life gets too boring.

## Challenges

As a natural actor, you can "fake it till you make it," which is wonderful when you are launching your career or moving into fresh territory. You can take on the nuance and pattern of the person you intend to be, but if this becomes a subconscious response to insecurity, it's hard to step off stage. You like to shine and can find teamwork challenging without a leadership role. You like a little routine, but you don't do well when you're bored. If life is too mundane or familiar, you can instigate drama. Once someone has proved to be disloyal, all bets are off. You react intensely to a betrayal of trust, wounding of pride, or feeling ignored. If you grow cynical, you can get manipulative, but this undermines the love you truly want.

## Primary emotional need

You came here to live wholeheartedly and on a larger scale. You may have grown up either in a family with a fair amount of emotional drama unfolding, so life felt like a play with a questionable author, or with a family that did not feel their life was exciting enough and tended to seek emotional outlet

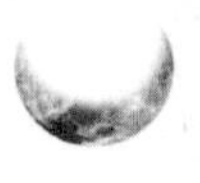

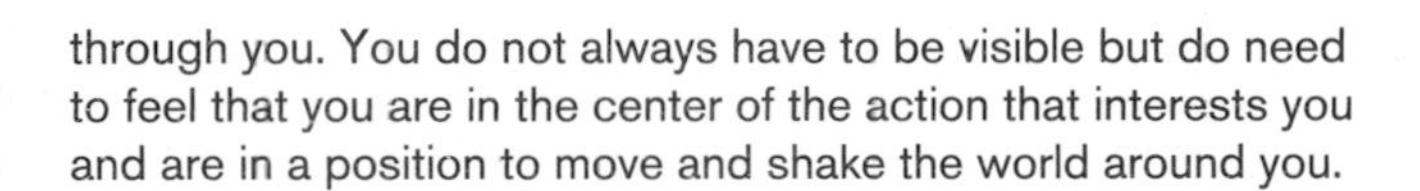

through you. You do not always have to be visible but do need to feel that you are in the center of the action that interests you and are in a position to move and shake the world around you.

## Dealing with those born under a Leo Moon

Leo Moons need to feel appreciated and valued. Criticism needs to be slipped in between honest points of appreciation to be heard easily. Anything they do that garners attention, and it doesn't really matter if it's good attention or bad attention, will tend to grow. Shine on any attribute that you want to grow and withdraw attention from problematic habits. They can be more stubborn and fixed in their ways than it first appears; collaborate on environmental changes and work toward healthy habits together.

**At work** If Leo Moons feel truly appreciated, they will shine for you. Work with their charisma and leadership capacities, put them at the head of the committee, at the front desk, schmoozing and charming, leading or being the point person. They can be great fund-raisers, promoters, performers, teachers, or motivational speakers. They prefer event-oriented work.

Sincere flattery will get you far with Leo Moon bosses. Show them how your success makes them look good.

**In romance** A Leo Moon needs to know that he is the most important person in your life. Never ever take Leo Moons for granted. Be happy to see them when they come home, and remember the grace notes–rose petals in the bathwater or extra décolletage in the dress. Never let them doubt your loyalty or test their pride. Argue in private only. Don't expect to win an argument through bluster or stubbornness; instead, work with the fact that

they want to make you happy and want to be loved. They collect attention and love from others, but are fundamentally loyal. Let them flirt–just remind them to bring their fine self home.

**In the family** Leo Moon children need warmth, consistency, and a clear reward pattern. Be tender with their pride, avoid criticism in public, but don't let them blackmail you with the threat of a tantrum. Engage their imagination with great adventures where they can identify with the hero or heroine.

Leo Moon parents need a specific role in any family function or they could take over the whole event. Make sure to live out your own dreams and not theirs.

Older Leo Moons may like to reminisce about their glory days and want a visiting schedule so they can look forward to the knock on the door.

# Gifts of a Leo Moon

**Warmheartedness:** A Leo Moon wrote the book on natural generosity. Once you understand what others need, you can share freely. You honestly want to see people happy.

**Loyalty:** Kindhearted and generous with friends, you need to know they have your back. You are capable of emotional intimacy with a truly loving heart, but may have to learn to trust that your beloveds want to see the true you.

**Charisma and leadership:** You can hold our attention for the common good, a skill that every teacher or team leader needs.

**Panache:** You have a natural sense of style that brings life to any room or gathering.

**Heart-centered strength:** You can be the pillar, the heartbeat of a family or a country, and can inspire and strengthen the people you serve.

**Skill in an emergency:** Your love of drama and adrenaline allows you to come alive in difficult circumstances that might be too stressful for others.

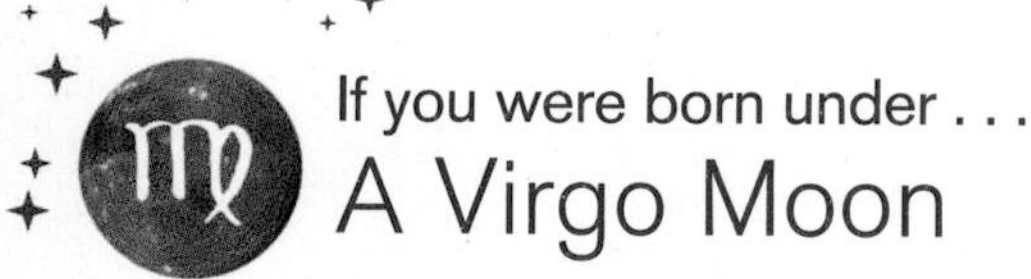

If you were born under . . .

# A Virgo Moon

You are likely to be verbal, witty, a natural mystery-seeker and problem solver, a cultural critic able to weave magic with words. Advice is your way of sharing love. You analyze and investigate for fun and profit, but can sometimes overanalyze your emotional experience and need to learn to trust your feelings. Your physical sensitivities are heightened, so you may feel better with a clean diet, subtle herbs, and hands-on healing, and you can become a skilled healer using these things.

The symbol for Virgo is a woman holding a sheaf of wheat, grain, and chaff together. Work with that metaphor. On a bad day, a Virgo Moon can obsess about the chaff, about life's problems, waste, and mistakes. When you can shift that focus toward the nutritious grain, all that's right with the world, you can guide the rest of us with intelligence and practical compassion.

## Challenges

You may become self-conscious because you scrutinize yourself so thoroughly that it can be hard to imagine that others see your gifts (and you have so many), not your faults. You can be anxiously aware of potential problems until you learn to relax and see the perfection that already exists. You can be a true introvert, needing time alone, away from taking care of others, or with those few beloveds who don't judge you. Since your health and soul really are sensitive, you may have habits, diets, or rituals that look neurotic to others, but are just your way to feel in control and relaxed. You may need to analyze relationships as a way to create intimacy when others are thinking more of poetry.

## Primary emotional need

You naturally understand the Japanese concept of *kaisen*, which translates as good change and means an effort at constant thoughtful improvement. You may have been born into a family that had a critical edge. Maybe your family felt that if they polished you, the rest of the world would be good to you, but that attitude may have left you with the feeling that you would never be good enough. You can learn to celebrate the beauty of this moment and still work to improve the next.

## Dealing with those born under a Virgo Moon

The lighter the touch you use with Virgo Moons, the better. Criticism only activates their considerable defenses; instead, define the problem and let them find a solution. Be generous with sincere praise only–they have an excellent radar for nonsense. They care deeply about people, and are often wonderful social critics and human rights activists, but they may have trouble balancing their needs and the needs of others unless they have solitude. Organizing and sorting can be relaxing for them, but, contrary to popular opinion, it isn't always their idea of a good time. Neatness is optional, cleanliness is not.

At work If you tell them off, they'll send you an itemized list of grievances. Work with their gifted critical and healing capacities; if they complain, put them at the head of the committee to analyze and solve the problem. Virgo Moon bosses can sound more critical than they really feel. You may need to ask them to list the things about your performance they like and what you should build upon.

**In romance** Sometimes Virgo Moons can feel cold and distant, but this is only reserve. Virgo is a passionate earth sign, but Virgo Moons are careful where they activate that fire. They are wary of commitment because they don't easily trust the perceptions of a lover and never want to be bored in a relationship. Slowly build adventurous trust together. Engage their intelligence. If they get prickly, rub their feet, walk in nature, help them to get out of their head . For pure bliss, take a bath together in candlelight or indulge in a weekend at a spa.

**In the family** Children born under a Virgo Moon worry. Don't dismiss their concerns, but help them to feel safer. Read with them and help them to connect their thoughts to their world. Virgo Moon parents share advice as a sign of love and a product of their anxiety, rather than an accurate assessment of you. Honor their efforts and reassure their anxiety.

As they age, Virgo Moons need healthy food and detailed projects to engage their industrious mind.

# Gifts of a Virgo Moon

**Gut intuition:** Quite literally, you can sense problems and opportunities by how your gut responds to the situation. Ignore your belly and it can scream; pay attention and it whispers to you.

**Work ethic:** You are happy when you love your work and may need a job to do when you first get to the party.

**Curiosity:** As a child, you took a clock apart to figure out how it worked. You may find vacations more fun if they have an educational slant and can get out of bed to Google a burning question.

**Writing:** Perception and communication are your magical tools.

**Listening:** You help other people unpack their soul and understand what needs fixing.

If you were born under . . .

# A Libra Moon

Beauty isn't something extra for you; it's an intrinsic need, like a Japanese aesthetic. A flower placed just so can be as beautiful to you as rich brocade or luxurious materials. Your appreciation for balance extends to all things–a balanced diet, equitable chores, balance between work and play. There's an abstract quality about Libra, even though it's ruled by romantic Venus. It's one of the few signs that has a nonliving object as a symbol, the scales. You hold those scales.

## Challenges

You can form a natural bridge between two sides, able to see inherent worth in each one, and comprehend both sides of a debate, but this can leave you indecisive. You avoid conflict and get a stomachache when caught between arguing people. When someone asks you where to go for dinner, you tend to say, "I don't know, where do you want to go?" because you honestly care more about the warmth of your interaction than you do about what you eat that night. When things go really wrong, you can reek of cynicism, not because you are truly pessimistic, but because you are indulging in the bitterness of the disappointed optimist. This will pass when you find just one thing beautiful, one spark to revive your natural hopefulness.

## Primary emotional need

If you were born under a Libra Moon, you came here to learn about relationships, justice, fairness, and keeping the peace. You may have been born into a family with strong opinions or

personalities and found yourself caught in the middle, trying to make everyone happy and help them to see one another's point of view. Perhaps you are giving up on all that and going your own way. Alternatively, your family might have been uncomfortable with conflict. You may hate to fight for personal reasons, but will fight for truth, justice, beauty, and the Libran way. Learn how to be both equitable and direct, and to live a life that is both balanced and decisive.

## Dealing with those born under a Libra Moon

Do not argue around your Libra Moon friends; don't put them in the middle. Make as much of an effort to see their point of view as they do yours. Respect their insight into the people around you. Without gossip, they'll know the people who are secretly seeing each other, who's arguing, and who's got problems at home. Although they appear very flexible, do not ask them to compromise on their art form or the issues closest to their souls.

**At work** Listen to the unusual perceptiveness about human relationships shown by Libra Moons. Point them toward mediation, human resources, welcoming the public, and design. Don't make them the first one to deal with irate customers, but ask for their help to write a diplomatic response.

Libra Moon bosses hate to police the people under them and need your cooperation as they constantly adjust and fine-tune the work.

**In romance** In love, Libra Moons have a secretly poetic soul and relationships can be consuming. They want their companion to be both excited by the art form of romance and interested in a fair and equitable relationship. Show a healthy sense of

compromise and an ability to disagree with kindness, respect, and a real curiosity about one another's perspective. Find out what they find beautiful and share the experience together, whether at art openings, concerts, or in beautiful landscapes.

**In the family** Libra Moon children can feel responsible for the emotional balance in the family, so let them know you will solve problems together and they don't have to be the peacemaker. Feed their creative soul and encourage their altruistic action. They can become hopeless if they feel the world is an ugly place and they don't have a way of affecting or improving it.

Libra Moon parents can help you to navigate the social world but will be uncomfortable if you take on family tensions with them.

Older Libra Moons may need your help to ascertain what they need and how to acquire it.

# Gifts of a Libra Moon

**Diplomacy:** You are naturally inclusive and are willing to explore another person's point of view. You can be an ambassador within your social sphere, helping one person understand another, one group understand the other.

**Fairness and even-handedness:** Since you are naturally at home in a balanced world, you notice when that balance is out of whack, when the situation is unfair or ugly, and want to make it right.

**Pacifism:** You would prefer a path of peace and cooperation.

**Natural leadership:** When mediation and diplomacy do not work, you can lead a direct, clean, and open confrontation and win in a court of law or court of public opinion.

**Artistry:** You have a natural sense of composition and beauty, although it may be quirky and individualistic it can make beauty out of a difficult situation.

**Romance:** No matter how pragmatic the rest of your chart, within your soul is a romantic poet.

If you were born under . . .

# A Scorpio Moon

Intense, stubborn, and soulful, you can appear self-contained or aloof because you're so private about your inner world. You may be arrogant about your particular field of expertise, but that comes from experience. Your ability to focus can be your gift and your curse, depending upon where you choose to direct it. You usually need time alone when you hurt, room to dive into your pain or depression, and then transform yourself as you come out the other side. You may find yourself bothered by small things but have the strength to endure experiences that would break others. As you become a well-adjusted Scorpio Moon, you find ways of communicating when you need solitude without pushing others away.

## Challenges

You do not suffer fools lightly; collaboration can be challenging for you and a frontier to your personal growth. Your temper can be formidable, an inner volcano; the more you suppress the temper, the bigger the pyroclastic blast when you explode. Your perception, intensity, and irony mean that even a casual, critical comment from you can be devastating. People are drawn to you, but if you scald them, they may not be back. Consider practicing, "This doesn't work for me," instead of, "You're an idiot." You may assume that beloveds also need solitude and leave them alone when they could use a hug. Be curious about their needs. Since emotional intimacy is so complex for you, it can be easier to reach out through sexuality than through conscious connection, but you transform when you have both.

## Primary emotional need

You came here to dive deeply into your interests, become comfortable with your own company, and live intensely. You may have experienced moments of isolation as a child, when your mother was distracted and you felt you had to rely on your own resources. Over your life, you learn how to have both intense connection and time for your own soul's journey.

## Dealing with those born under a Scorpio Moon

Mysterious Scorpio Moons can be attractive and tricky to work with, but usually worth the effort. They can be like a cat that wants to be petted, until they don't, and then they scratch. Respect their privacy. Scorpio Moons develop habits that can appear obsessive-compulsive, but are just their own form of meditation. They need a few core possessions only, and don't want to share them, whether that's food, mates, or a favorite chair.

**At work** Help Scorpio Moons find a niche where concentration and investigative skills are appreciated, and where their prickly edges are not inconvenient. Let them do what they're good at, and don't ask them to broaden their interests. They can be geniuses at work but still need remedial interpersonal coaching. They work best independently, but can then report back to a group. If the boss has a Scorpio Moon, don't take sharp comments personally, but do clarify priorities. Stay on track and prove you can work on your own.

**In romance** Don't try to understand them—they like being a mystery. Find healthy ways of working with them instead. If you are loved by a Scorpio Moon, you will be loved with intensity and purpose. These people can be possessive, often demanding.

They appreciate your independence, but when you are interacting with them, they want your whole attention. Don't even joke about infidelity or finding someone else attractive. They will not be amused. If they get prickly, walk away before you get too hurt and come back to the subject later.

**In the family** Scorpio Moon children need time around other interesting and introverted children. They should not feel forced to engage or show off.

Do not talk down to them, but share what makes you curious. If you want to know how they feel, inquire tangentially rather than directly–maybe have them help you tell a story about a child in a similar circumstance.

Scorpio Moon parents need respect. Their extremely firm opinions have to be accepted, if not necessarily agreed upon, and they require clear boundaries for both sides.

Older Scorpio Moons need solitude without isolation.

# Gifts of a Scorpio Moon

**Depth and complexity:** No one would ever call you shallow, or ever truly know the far corners of your psyche. In your depths you connect to a primal understanding, which can pour into your creative process.

**Curiosity:** You are a true investigator and researcher. You look under rocks, in the back of caves and closets, and behind the scenes to see what is really going on.

**Concentration:** When one question or topic grabs you, the headlight beam of your mind will hold until you have an answer. Be careful what you obsess about. If it's hard to stop obsessing about an ex-love, give yourself something else to concentrate upon. You are a natural with formal meditation.

**Self-direction:** You work best when the inspiration comes from within.

**Primal energy:** You have about you a charismatic sensuality. Like moths to a flame, people can be drawn to your intensity and mystery. When you truly commit, you can become a rock-solid touchstone for your family.

If you were born under . . .

# A Sagittarius Moon

By nature you're optimistic, expansive, and adventurous with an allergic reaction to being contained or curtailed. You may identify as a global citizen or feel most at home with travelers of the mind, body, or spirit. It's always good for you to know you could travel. When the doors are open, it's easier for you to stay.

You are comfortable when you can express yourself–laugh loud or sit quietly as the mood strikes you, play drums at midnight if you like, and seek your own spiritual truths. You may be seen as tactless because you are so honest and direct, but actually you are naturally empathic to humans and animals alike. Although you enjoy friendly debate, you prefer to avoid direct confrontation and would rather improve your world through law, education, or just by leaving town.

## Challenges

Your challenge is to embrace your eternally youthful spark while releasing immaturity. A feeling of claustrophobia may engulf you in emotionally or physically closed spaces. You may prefer to drive yourself to the party so you can leave when you want–you are happy to stay as long as you're free to go. For the same reason, you can have a fear of commitment, but can learn to trust. When life gets difficult, you may be tempted to take a geographic cure, figuring that a new location will solve the problem. It may be great medicine, but wherever you go, there you are, and you still need to work through the problems. You might carry a collection of books or travel paraphernalia that would feel like clutter to some but mean home to you.

## Primary emotional need

You came here to explore. You may have been raised by people who didn't conform to the normal adult parental role–a parent may have left and set the paradigm for travel, or felt more like a sibling or buddy than a mom or dad. The message came through subtly that ordinary family and social roles could be trapping, and freedom was a most desirable trait.

## Dealing with those born under a Sagittarius Moon

Appreciate their disarming honesty, adopt a playful spirit, and explore with them. It won't work to disagree directly, confine them, or limit their palette. They'll become like a wild animal and look for the door. Be disarmingly real and transparent with them. They accept quirks as long as they feel you're not hiding anything.

**At work** The longer the leash you give your Sagittarius Moon employee, the happier and more productive he/she will be. If you have international accounts, need someone who can travel at a moment's notice, be at home with people from any socioeconomic class, or speak difficult truths without a barbed edge, look for your Sagittarius Moon.

Sagittarius Moon bosses won't micromanage, but need to trust the integrity of their employees completely.

**In romance** Take your Sagittarius Moon sweetie to listen to African music one night, a science lecture the next, with French food in between. Hike together. Ride horses or cavort with a dog. Give Sagittarius Moons unique and exotic presents, which don't need to be expensive. Trust their restlessness. They don't crave other people's attention; they crave breadth of experience and

have a phobia of being trapped in a bad relationship. Laugh together often and ask probing questions. Be completely honest. If Sagittarius Moons smell even a hint of obfuscation or denial, they lose trust. As long as the doors are open, they'll walk with you while you explore together, handle conflict with kind honesty, and settle into dear companionship.

**In the family** Sagittarius Moon children need spontaneous adventure. Weave that sense of daring into everyday life. Invent games at the corner park, children's library, and the zoo. Take them on a hike and introduce them to bugs. Just take them with you wherever you go. They are usually great travelers. Encourage their questions and teach them tact about when to speak up and when to wait.

Forgive Sagittarian parents their frank honesty. If they don't like your hair or your beau, they'll say so.

For older Sagittarius Moons, mobility is key.

# Gifts of a Sagittarius Moon

**Gratitude:** If you were put in a barn full of manure, another might focus on the mess but you would look for the horse. You make the best of each situation or move on quickly.

**Cheerfulness:** You have a real need to remain wryly humorous or optimistic, no matter what the odds, and that hopefulness can be contagious.

**Connection with nature:** You feel at home with wild creatures under the starry skies or with furry friends at home. You have a spiritual connection to nature and can be an advocate for our ecosystem.

**International curiosity:** You want to know about other cultures, ideas, and languages and are attracted to people with foreign accents. You feel at home in the company of travelers. Your curiosity draws you to travel in your mind, through books, and philosophic or metaphysical explorations.

**Honesty:** You say it like you see it and may speak for the people around you who are too diplomatic or upset to speak the truth.

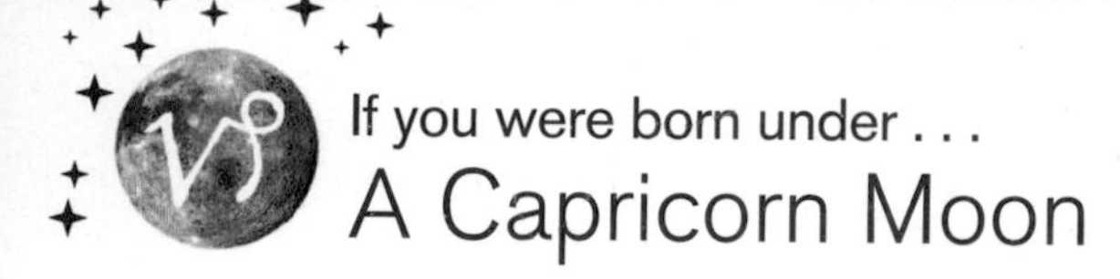

# If you were born under . . . A Capricorn Moon

You prefer to be organized and in control and have a natural reserve that can seem cool to some and cold to others. Actually, your feelings run strong and deep like an underground river.

Your work is such a part of your identity, whether it's a paid job or chosen family role, that it's important to make it right. When you love your work, you have more resilience and room in your heart for the rest of your life. You need a regular sense of accomplishment, so work toward short-term goals that accrue into your long-term dreams. When in doubt, make a list, check it off as you go, and watch your mood improve.

## Challenges

You often have good ideas about what needs to be done, so it's easier for you to be the manager, or work for yourself, than it is to take direction, unless you really respect the boss. You may be your own harsh critic, and when you're hard on yourself, you can be judgmental of others. When you have high expectations of yourself, you can be daunted by how far you have to go and get depressed. It can be challenging for you to access and express your feelings, creating an existential loneliness. If you soften your judgment and look at yourself and others kindly, you can find it easier to connect and to live up to your amazing potential.

## Primary emotional need

You may have come from a long line of competent people who tended to judge themselves and others by what they do, not who they are. Your parents may have worked and cooked for

you rather than sat down and played, or your family may have been distracted by events and left you to organize your own life. You have a journey to take this lifetime, places to go and things to do, but you need to learn that you matter just by being present. Ask yourself those questions you weren't asked as a child. How do I feel? What do I need? What makes me happy? Once you can do this for yourself, you can do the same for your beloveds.

## Dealing with those born under a Capricorn Moon

Don't dismiss a Capricorn Moon. Anyone born under this Moon tends to treat others with respect and wants it in return. If you come in crying, Capricorn Moons won't offer just a sympathetic hug–they'll want to form a plan and solve the problem. If you just need to process what's happened and complain, do so elsewhere. You will rarely need bail money for Capricorn Moons. They're highly competent, rational thinkers, and generally risk-averse. If they do go on the dark side, they won't be caught easily.

**At work** Deal with work first, socialize later. Capricorn Moons don't need bragging, they just need competence. Develop long-range plans and mission statements with them and refer back to them often. Forgive their control issues and keep clean boundaries between your work and theirs, or they can take over. If they work under you, encourage pride in their work and grow leadership capacities with small projects marked by clear expectations. For Capricorn Moon bosses, respect their authority but question process.

**In romance** Still rivers run deep. Capricorn Moons may appear self-contained but often could really use a hug. Preoccupations about self-worth and self-doubt can make them

emotionally unavailable until they prove themselves. Don't confuse their quiet coping skills with a willingness to be taken for granted, nor their independence with a lack of warmth. They find it romantic to work together. If you want them to relax with you, let them know you respect their work, they're safe and don't have to be in control, and that it's time to kick back.

**In the family** Children born under a Capricorn Moon are never quite sure their parents have it together. Reassure them that you're the alpha and have their security in mind. Spend time together and ask questions about how they feel and what they need, so they learn to ask those questions of themselves.

Capricorn Moon parents can be controlling. You may want to tell them to leave your schedule alone.

Older Capricorn Moons need to feel they are captain of their own ship for as long as possible.

# Gifts of a Capricorn Moon

**Leadership:** Once you build your confidence, you have true executive ability and are capable of managing other people, even if they don't want to be managed.

**Common sense:** You have uncommonly good common sense. Don't be surprised if your friends are less practical.

**Competitiveness:** You compete with your own personal best. You don't mind others winning the game, you just hate to lose. Tap into that desire for the motivation to improve yourself and your circumstances—just take it one step at a time.

**Coolness:** Your controlled emotions can make you look attractively cool, calm, and collected under stress. You can be the most levelheaded person in a real crisis. Emergencies activate your adrenaline-inspired competence.

**Architecture:** Work with your unusual ability to see spatial relationships and your pragmatic design sense to create functional and organized surroundings.

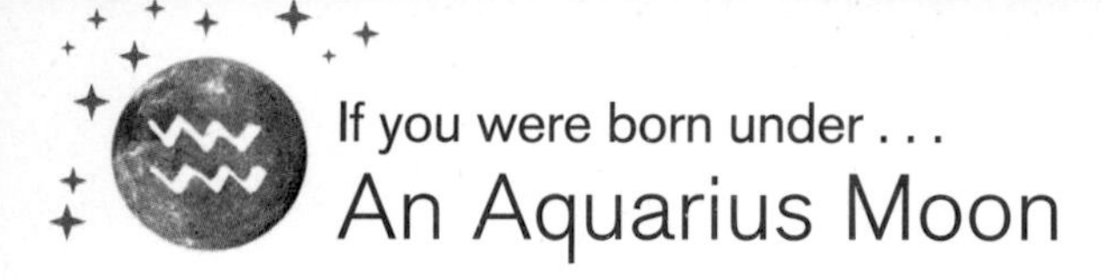

If you were born under . . .

# An Aquarius Moon

You know about group dynamics. Friendly, humanitarian, original, idealistic, those people born under an Aquarius Moon can't wait to get on their white horses and go save the world, and this habit can be both a gift and a challenge. You may not always choose to gallop off on a mission because of your natural eccentricity. It's not that you think outside of the box so much as that you don't really acknowledge the box's existence.

## Challenges

Although you are remarkably curious and open-minded, you can develop a stubborn opinion or theory that makes it difficult for you to see fresh evidence. You can also assume that everyone would be happier engaging the group and miss cues from the retreating introverts nearby. Your naturally philosophical bent can develop a wacky theory and try to cram your experience into it. Your farsightedness can be so focused on the horizon that you miss the sensitive feelings of the individuals closest to you. You can get abstracted from your own emotions, so your challenge is to become authentically aware of your true feelings and learn to stay intimately connected with others.

## Primary emotional need

You came into this life to understand the individual's place within the group. You may have been born into a family that is more aware of how the clan works than how they feel themselves. You may have been raised in a large family or feel like you were raised by the community. Perhaps your parents asked, "What would the neighbors think?" or "What does the world need?" instead of "Does that make you happy?" To use this training well in group dynamics without being limited by it, you need to let go of other people's ideals to find your own true philosophy, and then live by that.

## Dealing with those born under an Aquarius Moon

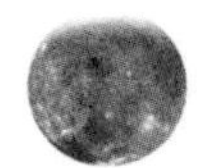

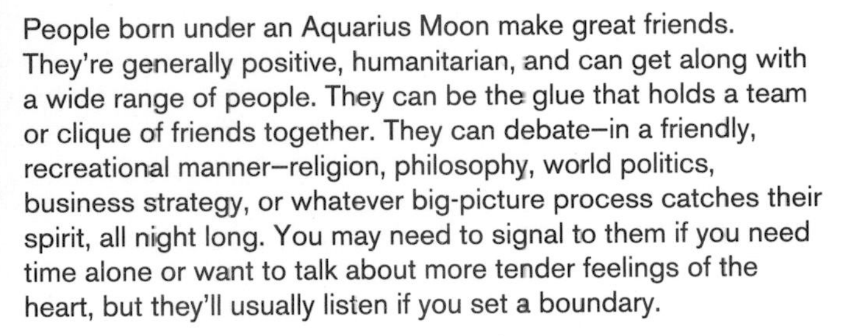

People born under an Aquarius Moon make great friends. They're generally positive, humanitarian, and can get along with a wide range of people. They can be the glue that holds a team or clique of friends together. They can debate–in a friendly, recreational manner–religion, philosophy, world politics, business strategy, or whatever big-picture process catches their spirit, all night long. You may need to signal to them if you need time alone or want to talk about more tender feelings of the heart, but they'll usually listen if you set a boundary.

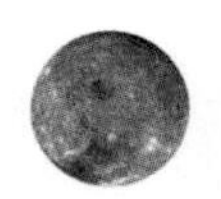

**At work** Many ministers, politicians, and union leaders were born under an Aquarius Moon. Put your Aquarius Moon people on the front line with all collective activities, and have them manage the office, coordinate the team or run the training or your social networking. Use them to help figure out what the workers need, what the public wants. They want to know why they're doing what they're doing; they need to understand the big picture, the theory first.

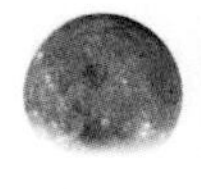

Aquarius bosses want to feel that the team works under them without contention.

**In romance** Romance? What romance? People born under an Aquarius Moon can forget what they or their beloveds need. Sometimes they want reminding, but never guilt-trip them for

time spent with their community; this is core to them. Instead, find what they are passionate about and share those moments. They love to participate in collective experiences—a dance club, a game, a political rally. Take them to an event in a room full of people with enthusiasm swelling, look deeply in their eyes, and let that excitement rub into the relationship.

**In the family** It's good for Aquarius Moon children to be involved in several different circles, their class at school, a team sport, and a painting class, for example. This will grow their talent for diversity, team leadership, and independence and give them a wide range of feedback for their self-understanding.

Aquarius Moon parents may want the family to do things together more than the individual members want to participate. You may need to get them used to the idea that you love them but aren't showing up for every Sunday dinner or campaign speech.

Older Aquarius Moons may thrive in assisted living quarters or a senior community, a place where both privacy and socializing are easily accessible.

# Gifts of an Aquarius Moon

**Networking:** You know somebody who knows somebody who has the answer. The Internet is home turf to your way of thinking—you can cross-reference and introduce people to just the resources and connections they need.

**Farsightedness:** You naturally look to the far horizon. You want to see the big picture and notice how your personal decisions may affect the world around you.

**Extroversion:** You can be an extrovert in the true sense of the word. Although you do need some time alone, you recharge from positive encounters with other people and have a way of making strangers feel at home.

**Innovativeness:** You are at home exploring possibilities and finding a fresh approach or new system. It can be easier for you to invent a new way than to remember how it used to be done. Embrace your iconoclastic imagination and find solutions that other people miss.

**Ability to philosophize:** You have a philosophical bent to your soul, for better or for worse. Make sure your philosophy is grounded in real experience and true perception, and then let it lead your life.

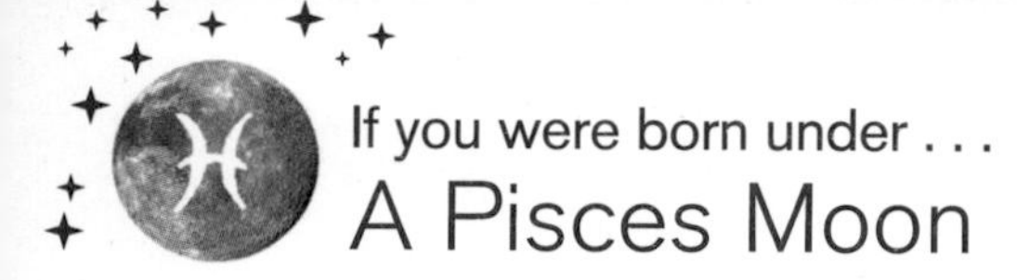

If you were born under . . .

# A Pisces Moon

✦ You are creative, perceptive, and flexible, and have deep inherent soul strength. You may be a true introvert because you pick up so much with your wonderfully intuitive antennae that you need time alone to recharge. If you're feeling too amorphous or emotional, it can help to invoke your Virgo counterpart. Showering or swimming can clear your energy field, while organizing and sorting can help strengthen your boundaries.

You may appear to dither before you make a decision because you synthesize so much information on so many levels. But when all parts of you agree, your decision is usually right on.

## Challenges

"You're fine. How am I?" The old joke between psychics holds true for you. You may not know your own emotions but you will know what everybody else is feeling. You can be uncertain where your stories end and another person's begin, which can lead to a cycle of codependency. When you get defensive, you can intuitively, unconsciously, sting where it hurts the most. Sometimes life can feel like sandpaper on raw nerves and you need to withdraw for self-care. You may have to walk out of a movie or leave a crowded environment if it's discordant with your mood. Your challenge is to train yourself to tune sensitively to joy, beauty, and infinite possibilities.

## Primary emotional need

You came here to learn to trust your feelings. Somebody who cared for you as a child may have felt overwhelmed by his or her own emotions, or been uncomfortable expressing them, but you resonated with your family's unspoken sentiments and didn't understand why. If family members were uneasy with these feelings within themselves, they may have tried to talk you out of your perceptions. This pattern can leave you uncertain until you learn to test and trust your inner knowing.

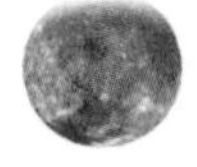

## Dealing with those born under a Pisces Moon

Highly intuitive, sensitive, and overwhelmingly creative, a person born under a Pisces Moon will always read your emotions, so don't even bother trying to hide how you feel. If you have to argue with Pisces Moons, sketch in the logic but share from the heart. You will get further if they empathize with your position. If you're upset or irritated with them, know that the lighter the touch you use, the more they can hear. If they don't seem to listen, their stillness may be a response to emotional intensity; give them time.

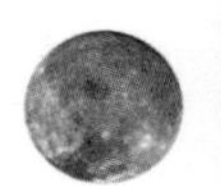

**At work** Trust Pisces Moon employees to know the conditions they need to do their best work. These can be pretty specific. They're worth it for their unusual ability to intuit how a project will unfold and to spot trouble a mile away. They synthesize information on many levels at once, which can make them wonderful managers, but they may prefer to lead from behind the scenes.

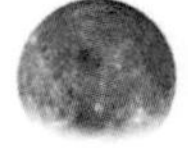

Don't mistake the thoughtfulness of Pisces Moon bosses for weakness, and do respond promptly to their well-considered specific requests.

**In romance** Pisces Moons like the grace notes, the romantic gestures, but rather than standard red roses, they want a sign that you have authentically considered what they prefer.

Most importantly, they need you to honor their emotions. Know when they're overloaded and need time alone. Encourage them to take care of themselves and not just be tuned into your needs. Dream with them and laugh together. Appreciate their delicate sensibilities, their tender heart, and the surprising steely strength underneath.

**In the family** Pisces Moon children need to have their reality and emotions honored and nurtured. Don't explain away their feelings. Help them to read their feelings, sort their hopes and fears from intuition, and make it easier for them to enjoy their imagination. Help them swoon into beauty, art, and the natural world.

Pisces Moon parents perfect worry as an art form. Take their anxiety as their form of love. Respect their concerns, but show them that you will find your own way.

Older Pisces Moons need a network of support.

# Gifts of a Pisces Moon

**Charm:** If you choose (and that can be a big if), you can be charming, eloquent, considerate. You know just how to reach any person you meet.

**Psychic sensitivity:** You may be unusually open to ghosts, spirits, and the environmental atmosphere. You perceive people's energy and intentions. Study basic psychic protection and grow more comfortable with this skill. Take some meditative time to become permeable to the universal spirit to return refreshed and inspired.

**Perception:** Your intuition and awareness of nuance make you a wonderful counselor, diplomat, or translator. No one can choose a gift better than you can.

**Lie detection:** You are painfully aware when a person's words don't match your perceptions of his or her feelings and wonder if that person is lying, hiding something, or distracted and troubled.

**Imagination:** Your imagination is a rich and bubbling wellspring–consciously tap into it. But if you get an intuitive hit and don't have the facts, you can invent a story to explain the feelings and head off base. Be aware of that fine line between intuition and imagination.

# Part II
# Navigate Your Day with the Moon

Explore the meaning and usefulness of the sign of the Moon each calendar day to help navigate your day and make the most of your time.

Navigate your day with . . .

# The Moon in Aries

A cardinal fire sign, Aries' fresh, rash enthusiasm is symbolized by a headstrong ram. When the Moon travels through Aries, we feel our life force rise up, our patience diminish, and our attitude sharpen. It's up to us to use the enthusiasm to revive our life and add in patience and foresight to soften the rough edges.

## The mood under an Aries Moon

Energized, brash, brusque, direct, independent, rebellious, and generous, but not empathetic. Feelings spike like lightning and dissipate quickly. We may feel astoundingly lazy when we're not motivated, but can throw ourselves into any action that excites us. Spontaneity renews our life force. The attitude on the street can be pugnacious and willful when met with resistance, but enthusiastic and direct otherwise. People tend to dress with less fuss and more practicality. They need to be able to move easily in what they're wearing and do what needs to be done.

Our inner adolescent activates, so instead of giving direct orders (which just set off our rebellious streak) it's better to speak in "I" terms, state the problem, and ask for help to solve it. If you have to deal with a particularly pugnacious personality during an Aries Moon, consider using reverse psychology—either start doing whatever it is badly in front of the person and bet him he can't do it, or tell him it's not allowed. If you are the one with a suddenly pugnacious personality, find a way to move out of reaction and into action. Ask yourself what you truly want and need at this moment.

It's easier to work in short, intense bursts rather than long periods of deep concentration. If you're teaching children or

pitching a business proposal, break up focused mental activity with pointed dialog, concrete examples, or physical moves.

## Romance

Aries brings us back to center in ourselves, but this can drift occasionally into self-centeredness. We're not naturally empathic under the Moon in Aries, but we can be loving (if not terribly patient) once we understand the need. So don't take it personally if your beloved seems inconsiderate and self-directed. Give him room and he will come back grateful. When you come together, consider letting him talk first, but then feel free to speak. Don't wait to be asked. Express affection enthusiastically, spontaneously, and passionately.

## Contemplation/meditation

The Moon in Aries may not bring out our wisest or most mature self, but it does turn up the volume of our inner voice and helps us clarify our wants and needs. Once we know, we can negotiate for our needs and balance those with the needs of others. It can be hard to sit still in meditation during the Aries Moon unless we take it on as a challenge or feel deeply engaged in the question. It may help to meditate in an unusual place, set a short but urgent meditation time, or take a meditative approach to martial arts.

## Things to do

Launch projects or initiate any action that takes enthusiasm and gumption. Express independent thought. Move into new territory. Cut to the chase. Clear the air. Demolish. Move furniture, exert spurts of energy. Set healthy boundaries. Enjoy bursts of laughter. Make succinct proposals. Invite heroism. Be clear, crisp, and to the point.

## Garden

Weed, dig, relocate rocks, and deal with pests. Start new beds–just don't plant the seeds yet.

# What to watch out for

**Loss of impulse control:** Take a note of sudden impulses, but unless the consequences are clear, wait for the dust to settle before taking action.

**Temper spikes:** Notice when a situation starts to reach boiling point and get out of there. Take a break and come back later.

**Accidents created by speed or flammable conditions:** Sharp knives, explosives, pools of fuel, and contentious situations all need extra attention and safety.

**Flaming tortillas:** Enjoy quick cooking, but watch out for a tendency to burn food.

**The perception of self-centeredness:** If a person feels stuck between his own needs and another's, he'll tend to take care of his own first, so don't set it up as an either/or situation.

**Impatience:** Avoid situations where you have to wait in line or deal with annoying people.

Navigate your day with . . .

# The Moon in Taurus

Taurus is a fixed earth sign. Its solid, strong, comfort-loving energy is symbolized by a bull, an earthy, potentially fierce, territorial creature that becomes placid and friendly when standing in a clover-filled field with a mate nearby.

## The mood under a Taurus Moon

We slow down and become more aware. Our senses are heightened, our patience expands, and our stubbornness grows. We want to be comfortable and will tend to agree with anybody who helps us feel safer, more secure, more relaxed. We want people to indulge our senses and ease our path. Taurus is known for being materialistic, but that tendency is not so much money-oriented as a desire to protect and grow our resources. We want to take care of our resources. Help us to do that and we'll love you. Touch our stuff, or look like you might take our romantic partner, our money, our comfy seat at the meeting, and watch those bullish horns come out. Give us cuddly circumstances and comfort food that is tasty and covered in sauces; don't ask us to try something exotic at the moment.

Don't push the pace. We would rather move with our own steady rhythm. The mood on the street can be steadier; the rhythm of the crowd more even-keeled unless someone gets pushed. Then the Taurus horns show up.

## Romance

Cuddle. Keep expectations low and help one another to feel accepted. We want to feel safe and comfortable. Show

appreciation in concrete ways, with a great meal and loving touch, and with practical help. You know that household chore your loved one has been nagging you about? Do it. Have a pillow fight. If a debate starts, stay in there and keep a sense of humor. We want to know our beloveds can stand up for themselves and push back but still love us.

## Contemplation/meditation

Engage a gentle moving meditation, yoga, stretching, massage, bodywork. Contemplate the fact that the word material comes from the Latin word *mater*, which means "mother." Look for the breath of the divine in the flower and the taste of food, in a catlike stretch in the sunshine. Offer gentle practical support to others as a form of prayer.

## Things to do

Follow through on projects recently initiated. Get in a groove for work and keep the rhythm steady. Deal with circumstances that require patience and determination. Negotiate financial transactions while we are deeply aware of our financial worth, of costs and expenses, and want to grow our resources. Have a meeting at school or work where diplomatic stubbornness can help the cause. While we have such an acute sense of value, look for worthy antiques or a good bargain. Choose design elements, such as color and texture. Trust the stylist with a new haircut. Feed the senses; enjoy bodywork, gentle exercise, and a nice, long, hot bath.

## Garden

At the time of this most fertile Moon, we can plant and fertilize anything, any seed, bulb, sapling, egg, or idea we want to grow abundantly.

# What to watch out for

**Stubbornness:** Fixed signs work like cornstarch and water (mix some up if you haven't given it a try)—they become liquid and flow when allowed to find their own rhythm, but push them and they become solid. When someone is digging in his heels, chin set with determination, consider backing off and trying again later.

**Greed:** We love our stuff. The Taurus Moon can bring out the inner dragon of avarice. Shopping under a Taurus Moon can be dangerous, because we develop an intense longing for the most expensive product in the store.

**Possessiveness:** Our eyes can grow green with jealousy if we feel someone is poaching in on our romantic territory.

**Sloth:** The Taurus Moon helps us to stay grounded and keep up a steady rhythm—once we get going. It can be hard to get started. Creature comforts call us, the coziness of our bed or a luxurious moment in the sunlight beckon us.

**Overindulgence:** We can feel wonderfully sensual but may begin to crave extra bonbons and cashmere.

Navigate your day with . . .

# The Moon in Gemini

A mutable air sign, Gemini's humorous versatility and scintillating communication skills are symbolized by twins who are engaged in deep conversation.

## The mood under a Gemini Moon

Nervy, funny, open-minded, versatile, restless, and good for multitasking, if not for concentration. Our energy is more in our head, and less in our heart, unless we consciously keep them connected. We need to talk it out. We're better able to handle interruptions, less able to handle boredom. We can enjoy an increased ability to assimilate information and see connections and possibilities we hadn't noticed before. Sound means a lot to us. The tone of a voice, bird song, music, and the restless cityscape noises affect us. We may need brighter colors, material that moves, and light statement pieces.

## Romance

The Gemini Moon brings a playful, flirtatious quality and a spark to the eye. Whisper in the ear. Laugh in bed and share the morning newspaper. Enjoy the banter and dance, the conversation of body language. We're ready to talk about anything except commitment. It's easy to strike up a new relationship or add spark to an old one, but we may be tested with a passing distraction. Tell stories. Explore the neighborhood together. Let the conversation roam and develop with lightness and humor. Just know that some people enjoy the poetry of romance and may not mean everything they say.

## Contemplation/meditation

Read a favorite line of poetry or a paragraph from spiritual scripture. Then set a timer for ten minutes and put pen to paper. Write a stream of consciousness response and do not stop writing until the timer goes off. Ponder the meaning, perceptions, and ramifications for you. Read your response aloud. Think back on it in spare moments throughout the day.

## Things to do

Take advantage of these extroverted, outgoing days to check in with clients and friends. Talk to strangers who walk up and start a conversation with you–they may bring surprising information. Chat to the neighbors. Find out what everybody's doing.

Cross-pollinate, share information, edit, weed, network; just be kind and avoid gossip. Get on Facebook, interview, multitask. Check on your contacts, reach out and make a cold call. Check in with the team and make sure everybody's on the same page. Read short stories. Gather information. Disseminate information in short staccato sound bites. Promote. Use ambient humor and diplomacy to tackle otherwise tough and heavy subjects. Find just the right words. Edit in short chunks. Experiment. Write a graphic novel or other mixed-media adventure. Make suggestions at work. Just keep everything a dialog, not a monologue; think ping-pong not marathon. Keep presentations short and to the point, stay relevant to events at hand.

## Garden

Tend to the aerial parts of plants, harvest grains, pinch buds, prune and trim where you want to restrict a plant's growth and encourage it to keep its shape. Weed or read up about the garden; collect ideas for the future.

Navigate your day with . . .

# The Moon in Cancer

The characteristics of Cancer, a cardinal water sign, are sensitivity, self-protection, and emotional leadership. Its symbol is a crab. Soft and squishy on the inside, the crab is safeguarded by an outer hard shell and pincers, and it is capable of walking on the deep ocean floor.

## The mood under a Cancer Moon

The general feeling is both tender and guarded. We connect with our gentle side and may need to process emotional backlog. If we feel endangered by our vulnerability, if critique feels sharp or people's demands too intense, we get crabby. The Cancer Moon can bring out our defensive genius—we may want to nurture and protect our home, our homeland, or our corner of the office, and be as protective as a mother grizzly bear about our beloveds. We are less inclined to take emotional risks or to perform under judgment; instead, let us share from our comfort zone.

The Cancer Moon can bring out a needy side that craves extra reassurance or extra food. Creature comforts feel good. Our feelings may be deep-rolling waves, but we may not be able to talk about them. In order to understand us, read our body language, rather than listening to our words.

## Romance

Avoid helpful suggestions or anything that sounds like criticism. Keep interactions sweet, tender, cozy, comfortable; cuddle by a fireside and enjoy familiar foods together. Take a bath together,

# What to watch out for

**Short attention span:** We can all get temporary attention deficit disorder, so keep your point crisp, clean, and specific.

**Distraction:** Like a dog when a squirrel goes by, we get distracted easily by passing events or new lines of thought to follow. We love the stimuli.

**Low impulse control:** If we think it, we say it; if we see it, we do it.

**Gossip:** Our mouths can run away with us. What seems like a good story to us might be another person's tender secret.

**Shallow thinking:** Our minds can run like escape pods buzzing the surface of the planet, taking in a lot of new information but less interested in depth and long-term consequences.

**Nervousness:** We can get a little wound up. Remember that anxiety is often a misuse of imagination, and redirect that nervous energy. If sleep is fugitive as the hamster wheel of our mind spins, write out concerns, then reconnect mind, heart, and body before sleep.

scrub each other's backs. Be family to one another. Let your significant other feel treasured, safe in your affection, and appreciated. If a beloved appears reserved, assume he still loves you and just needs some time within. If you're in need of reassurance, ask for it simply and directly. Give a hug to get a hug.

## Contemplation/meditation

Notice what you are truly hungry for–is it love, connection, spirit? Reach in to that deeper hunger and ask what truly feeds you. Meditate on the idea that your true home is the whole of this Earth, which is our mother.

## Things to do

Be warm and considerate, respecting other people's boundaries exquisitely. Let coworkers know you will watch their backs; let the boss know you are doing your share of the work to make the business secure. Nurture and reassure coworkers and the people close to you; pour on positive feedback for everything they've done right. Feed people healthy, simple, comfort foods. Nurture causes you believe in, your homeland, and ecosystem. Nest, rest, recollect. Make your home feel more comfortable and safe; catch up with your paperwork. Bathe, cook, and hydrate. Listen to your gut instincts. Take some "shell" time, that is time within your sanctuary, and take care of yourself. Take a long, hot bath at the end of the day.

## Garden

Cancer is one of the most fertile Moons. It's time to water everything well. Turn your attention to edible plants and transplant, fertilize, nurture, and tend.

# What to watch out for

**Crankiness:** If we feel self-conscious or are not comfortable, it's all too easy to be irritable and start finding fault.

**Neediness:** We can become emotionally uncentered if we're not feeling safe and secure. Rather than asking others for reassurance, we may feel more grounded if we hold our own inner child carefully and lovingly. Once we remember we can take care of ourselves, we can accept other people's foibles and inconsistency with more grace.

**Overeating or undereating:** The sign Cancer rules the stomach and breasts, nurture in and out of the body. Watch a tendency for emotional eating, either too much or too little, in response to the emotional waves of the day.

**Self-consciousness:** Paradoxically, we may become less secure if we focus on ourselves and our vulnerabilities. We need to do our own emotional homework and then turn our attention to others, noticing their vulnerabilities and seeing what we can do to help.

**Codependency:** Nurturing others is a wonderful thing, but if we mother because it feels safer than being a leader, a lover, or taking care of ourselves, then we're stepping into codependency. Are we truly helping, or are we encouraging another person's weakness and disempowering our own self-care?

Navigate your day with . . .

# The Moon in Leo

A fixed fire sign, Leo's generosity, charisma, and drama are symbolized by a proud, strong, dominant lion.

## The mood under a Leo Moon

Open-hearted, generous, romantic, stubborn, and expressive. Our energy level can be catlike–we may prefer lazy stretches in the sunlight interspersed with great bursts of energy when we're emotionally engaged. We want to shine, to be appreciated, and may dress more dramatically than usual, with color and flair. Public interactions can feel like improvisational theater. Dinner can become a party, and a party can be legendary.

We may speak melodramatically to get our story across, but we really want to be understood. The Leo Moon encourages our generosity once we understand what's needed, but it can be challenging to get out of our own perspective and empathically walk in another's shoes.

## Romance

Ignore or take your beloved for granted and you will get in trouble. Share the spotlight rather than compete for it. Let him feel your heart shining. Feel free to dress up or show off. We like to be proud of our companions under the Leo Moon and we like them to be proud of us. It's a wonderful night for dinner and dancing, but even mundane meals can be made special with a little extra attention. If only for a few minutes, put your beloved at the center of your world, ask about his day, and tell him a few things you honestly appreciate about him.

## Contemplation/meditation

Hold in your heart the thought, "May I be happy, may I find joy, may I refrain from whatever prevents happiness." Then hold in your heart the same thought about a dearly beloved. Do the same for a friend, for a colleague, for a relative stranger, for starving children, for a world leader, for dangerous people, or an enemy. Let your heart shine out to the whole world, and then bring that attention back to yourself.

## Things to do

The Leo Moon brings an extra spark to performance, so schedule any presentation for this time, knowing you can pull it off with unusual flair and panache. Go see music or the performing arts. Show your boss how your work contributes to overall success, and ask for a raise. Tell a story. Do an interview and help someone tell their story. Compete with your own personal best. Promote. Help others feel special and appreciated, whether they are lover, client, or friend. Practice gratitude. Do anything that engages this temporary extroverted spirit; socialize, make a grand entrance, take dance lessons, go on a first date. Engage the leonine creativity to arrange, design, and celebrate. Celebrate each other's achievements at a family dinner.

## Garden

Cultivate, harvest, tend the flowers, work on the garden's design, and make sure plants get enough sunlight.

# What to watch out for

**Ego clashes:** We get easily miffed if we feel ignored or underestimated. Teamwork can suffer from individual grandstanding, and pride can trip us up or blind us to another's perspective.

**Unnecessary drama:** Ordinary chores can be a challenge. We can start trouble if we're bored or the world seems too mundane. We can speak in hyperbole if ordinary words just don't encompass the enormity of our feelings. Trust that a simple story can speak volumes.

**Self-centeredness:** A gift from the Leo Moon can be the sense that "I am the center of the universe, and so are you." The challenge can be the attitude that "I am the center of the universe, and you are not."

**Manipulation:** We can be manipulative just because it helps us to feel alive and powerful. We can be manipulated by effulgent compliments.

**Stubbornness:** We are open-minded when excited and feeling appreciated, but if directly opposed, we can really dig in our heels. Consider putting any ongoing argument aside and say, "I still disagree with you but care about you anyway." Rebuild connection and tackle the problem again in a few days' time.

♍ ♍ ♍ ♍ ♍

♍ Navigate your day with . . .

# The Moon in Virgo

Virgo is a mutable earth sign. Its nourishing and analytical abilities are symbolized by a woman holding a sheaf of wheat, a plant that needs to be sorted, chaff from grain, in order to be useful.

## The mood under a Virgo Moon

When the Moon travels through Virgo, our mind and attitude sharpen, our nervous system speeds up, and our work calls. Mischief may twinkle in our eyes as we see the foibles of the world around us. We see through bravado and prefer humble, practical action. The milieu is sensitive, health-oriented, compassionate, and particular; we may get a bit highly strung but we understand how details create the whole. An interesting paradox occurs—we are unusually good at critical thinking and understanding what needs to be fixed, and unusually bad at accepting criticism and suggestions. We can get so sensitive that it can be hard to stay in our hearts, and so we retreat to our active minds. But we need our heart and mind to work together to make the most of this Moon.

## Romance

First, we talk. To discuss work, the healing process, art, or whatever fascinates us in the world is wonderful foreplay under a Virgo Moon. See a play and argue its merits. We need to come together in the mind first. We just never critique one another, as we're unusually sensitive to criticism. Instead, find something specific you like about your companion, and let them know in detail. Share healthy food, shower together, dance,

walk, do couples yoga, or share other embodied action to get out of the mind only, and back into the body.

## Contemplation/meditation

Ponder the perfection of the world. It teaches us what we need to learn, grows our skills, challenges us to step up and make the world even better. Meditate on how this could be so, and how life has trained you for this.

## Things to do

Take great ideas brainstormed under the Virgo Moon and make them so. Analyze, edit, critique, organize, and have faith in the perfection of the whole. Assess the details, sort what to keep and what to release, but be very sparing with advice. Empathy and compassion take us farther and accomplish more. Deal with paperwork, mechanics, delicate crafts, or anything where precision is needed. Sort closets and clean the house. Honor health and health-related issues, work out, eat well; assess what supports health. Find healthy ways to use critical thinking skills, away from beloveds and coworkers. Weave magic to create better alternatives with your words as writer, speaker, teacher, and cohort.

## Garden

Weed, dig, relocate rocks, harvest, sort and store seeds, and deal with pests.

# What to watch out for

**Pickiness:** An unusual exactitude can be helpful in the right places—just watch a tendency to focus on the negative. Weed the garden, but remember that the point is to nurture and protect what we do want to grow. Play with that metaphor.

**Unwanted advice:** We gain new insight into the problem and what needs fixing, and we're happy to share that information, but unless advice is asked for, our generous and insightful bon mots will be heard as criticism.

**Being over critical:** We can easily see people's mistakes and foibles and can relish gossiping sessions about everything they're doing wrong, but that fun is short-lived and will come back to us. Write a scintillating movie critique, but maintain a kind lens closer to home.

**Self-criticism:** When we are critical of the world, we turn this perception inward, too, becoming unusually aware of our own foibles, and we grow self-conscious or insecure. We may feel unready and won't thank you for pointing any of this out.

**Indigestion:** Virgo rules the digestive tract, the ability to sort nutrient from waste, which is a great metaphor for all activities under the Virgo Moon. Focus on the nutrients. Eat and support the digestive system with light, healthy foods and probiotics.

Navigate your day with . . .

# The Moon in Libra

The cardinal air sign's friendly, egalitarian, humanitarian, and artistic nature is represented by a woman holding a balanced scale.

## The mood under a Libra Moon

Our attention shifts from work to relationships and a sense of aesthetics. The mood is sociable, flirtatious, pleasant, and interpersonally aware, but our relationship expectations can crank up. We feel it keenly if our beloveds aren't available to interact when we're ready to do so. People are generally friendly on the streets and tend to let others through the doorway first. We appreciate etiquette and kindness. We are open to debate but not interested in confrontation.

## Romance

If you are single, it's a good night to do something you love and see who's out there doing it too—people are companionable and unusually approachable, if a little shy, under the Libra Moon. Don't be too aggressive, seduce gently.

In a long-standing relationship, share a burden or pursue a project together. Have a date night. Hold hands for no reason. Leave a love note. Slow dance in the kitchen. Speak sweet romantic words as you reach for one another. This is a good time to talk about the nature of the relationship, how to support your partnership, and where you are going together, but make it a gentle, open-ended exploration.

## Contemplation/meditation

Look for a deeper understanding of beauty. *Hozho* is a Navajo term for the balance of natural order, meaning the balance between the natural world around us, our soul, and our life journey. Contemplate hozho. Assess the balance between your work and your love life, between your needs and those of others. When we're walking in a good way, that is in a way fair to ourselves, to our beloveds, and to the world around us, we walk in beauty.

## Things to do

Take the blueprints created under the Virgo Moon and gather the human resources to put them into practice. It's a great time

to reach out, to make overtures, to pitch an idea that requires people skills and open minds. Have a party, or arrange a meeting where teambuilding is more important than decision-making. Our sense of aesthetics is heightened, so it's a good time to make design decisions, go shopping, have your hair done, or improve a website.

More fundamentally, the Libra Moon encourages us to seek a peaceful, egalitarian balance. Our sense of social justice heightens, and so does our outrage at unfair or unequal situations, from how we handle household chores to how we navigate the politics around us. "That's unfair" can become the battle cry. Go to court, mediate, attend legal meetings, meet clients, and negotiate contracts from a win-win perspective.

## Garden

Tend the flowers and the shape of the garden. Prune for beauty more than growth, check the pH balance of the soil, and investigate companion planting. Feed the birds.

# What to watch out for

**Indecisiveness:** The Libra Moon loans us the ability to see the merits of both sides, which is wonderful for opening our minds to possibilities, but can make even simple decisions, such as which soap to buy, problematic.

**Codependent behavior:** We may know what other people need more than we know what we need ourselves. Our goal must be a balance of our needs and theirs, not a choice between them.

**Conflict avoidance:** We just want everyone to get along peacefully, and may be unusually uncomfortable with confrontation or someone's sharp temper. We may allow bad behavior in the name of keeping the peace. Instead, we can agree to think about the other person's perspective, and defer any decision until the situation is clarified.

**Relationship obsession:** We can forget our work and socialize, or obsess over every nuance and phrase in the story of our relationship.

**Hurt feelings:** We can be taken by surprise because while we're feeling unusually open, another person may be feeling narky, and it can be a shock to the system. If so, step away rather than escalate.

Navigate your day with . . .

# The Moon in Scorpio

The focus and intensity of Scorpio, a fixed water sign, is represented by a phoenix and a scorpion. The phoenix, a legendary bird that rises from fire's ashes, represents the durable Scorpio ability to transform. The scorpion represents soft tenderness within, guarded by a hard shell and a stinger without.

## The mood under a Scorpio Moon

Attitude–don't leave home without it. Note the black boots and spiked heels, edgy versus frivolous attire. People are more serious, curious, introspective, introverted, investigative, cynical, suspicious, focused, and not interested in being interrupted. Don't waste our time with pleasantries, and don't set off our defenses recreationally. And don't mind if we need a little time alone in our cave. Sarcastic or dark humor is appreciated, as long as it's not directed at us.

We may be feeling both unusually curious and unusually private. We learn from intensity, depth, and power. Sexuality can be potent, musky. Our feelings may be so strong that we don't put them into words. Unspoken messages, come hither or stay away, echo through our body language. Eyes flash, tails twitch. Temper, passion, or bored indifference reflect in our movement.

## Romance

On the surface, conversation may be about politics, work, what's wrong with the world, but the body speaks another language. The Scorpio Moon does not encourage us to show vulnerability. Our feelings are so primal we may not feel comfortable talking

about them, so you need to read between the lines. People may be less casually flirtatious, but you will notice unspoken musky undertones. It can feel safer to think of sex rather than affection. Enjoy the ambient chemistry, just stay in touch with the more complex feelings underneath. We may need as much time alone as we do in connection, though. Don't take it personally.

## Contemplation/meditation

Underneath the turbulence of our lives lies the deep well that connects to spirit. Turn your curiosity inward and look for that connection. Drop beneath mental chatter, between the tossing winds of emotion, and down into the deepest wells of the soul. Contemplate the knowledge that every being you meet also has a deep connection to the source at the roots of their soul.

## Things to do

Research, investigate, and find out what's really going on. Adopt a plan and run with it. Let people work alone now and report back to the team later. To get us interested in your idea, pique our curiosity. Respect personal space, ask no invasive questions, and respect boundaries exquisitely.

Under the Scorpio Moon we focus easily. We can either obsess productively about our work, or we can tortuously obsess about some emotional conundrum. It's up to us. Direct this unusually durable concentration away from obsession and toward creation. Perform surgery, prune the deadwood, and eliminate waste.

The Scorpio Moon weaves the visible and invisible worlds together. Explore metaphysical ideas and paranormal phenomena. Investigate family history and talk to the ancestors. Take time alone to hear your own soul. Meditate.

## Garden

Dig deep in your garden, divide perennials, encourage pollination, plant seeds, make new plants from grafts, feed the soil, turn the compost, build watering trenches.

# What to watch out for

**Jealousy/possessiveness:** Do not toy with other people's emotions; it may get explosive. Revenge fantasies can show up, but we don't have to run with them. They indicate underlying pain that needs to be healed.

**Snappy comebacks:** That scorpion sting is all too easy to invoke, particularly if we feel our boundaries are crossed, or our relationships endangered; or we may just not suffer fools gladly.

**Obsession:** If we start to focus on something unproductive, such as what's wrong with our marriage or whether our lover looked at another person, we can't just let it drop. But we can replace it with a healthier obsession.

**Curiosity:** Remember the golden rule and only investigate in others' lives what you are willing to have investigated in your own. Do not jump to conclusions if you find an odd phone number in your partner's pocket. Keep an open mind.

**Isolation:** We all could use a moment of solitude but that doesn't mean isolation. Don't push others away–just be honest when you need some time alone.

Navigate your day with . . .

# The Moon in Sagittarius

The mutable fire sign signifying restless, cheerful, ruthless honesty is symbolized by a centaur, a being that is half human and half horse. The centaur connects humans with the nonhuman world and can run far and fast over the plains.

## The mood under a Sagittarius Moon

Honest, disarmingly tactless, spontaneous, outdoorsy, philosophical, playful, international, freedom-loving, and generally optimistic. It's time to drop the attitude and get real. We have a sudden allergy to lies, exaggerations, distortions of the truth, but may not agree with one another on what the truth actually means. We're willing to confront new ideas and tell you what we think of them directly, but we don't really want to argue. Sagittarius is the sign of the traveler and we want to travel in mind, body, or spirit, to explore some corner or concept we have yet to see.

## Romance

If you're single, get out there, engage the world, and see what sparks. If in a relationship, find a comfortable way to explore the world together. Take a hike, go to a foreign movie, enjoy world beat music, eat exotic food. Let the conversation range far and wide. Talk over the touchy points of your relationship with a light but honest touch. Enjoy being physical together–break a sweat as you dance or play racquetball. Wrestle and have a pillow fight, just keep your sense of humor. Cheerfully wave while your loved one sails away and greet him when he returns. Advice

from Kahlil Gibran: "Let there be spaces in your togetherness, and let the winds of the heavens dance between you. Love one another but make not a bond of love: Let it rather be a moving sea between the shores of your souls."

## Contemplation/meditation

Visualize a favorite place outdoors, whether that's a floral garden or rough seacoast–a place that makes you feel joyfully connected to the natural world. Notice the ground, sounds, smells, and the quality of the wind. Look around and see if there is a special treat or teaching waiting for you here. Notice how this place feels to your body and anchor the memory. Let your mind come back to this place often and easily when you need a taste of this Sagittarian expansiveness.

## Things to do

Break routine and take exercise–travel down a street you don't normally take, stop at an unusual coffeehouse, talk to someone whose perspective stretches your own, hike, talk to strangers, visit a dog park, whether or not you have a dog. Take your own transport to the party, because you'll want the freedom to stay or go as you please.

Check in with international contacts and politics. This is a good time to investigate new contacts or sources, reach out to new clients, make cold calls, or pitch a fresh idea to people with open minds. You will be able to show them how this idea has the potential to expand their horizons. Get people talking and they will tell you their secrets. Explore the joys and responsibilities of being a global citizen and support the rights and obligations of free speech. Make travel arrangements. Tease a friend and use playfulness to open the flow of communication. Reach across cultural boundaries. Find an open, frank, but unbarbed way of speaking a difficult truth. Move the body, dance, run, bicycle, feel the life force flowing.

## Garden

Harvest wild herbs and root vegetables. Cultivate the soil. Meander through other gardens and gather ideas. Find any good excuse to be outside.

# What to watch out for

**Wanderlust:** Yes we need to explore; just think twice before dropping work and walking off into the sunset.

**Tactlessness:** Forgive the grandmother who blurts out that she hates your haircut. Our filters go down and we speak what's on our mind. Say it like it is, but make sure it's not only true, but necessary and kind.

**Need for freedom:** Do not act possessively toward loved ones. Give them room to roam and they will love you for it. Conversely, don't run away and join the circus when all you really need is a walk around the block.

**Silliness:** Sagittarius brings a lighthearted break between two heavy Moon signs. We need the comic relief. We need to laugh and hear bitter truths with humor, but not everybody can take the teasing. Use tact.

Navigate your day with . . .

# The Moon in Capricorn

The vision and determined ambition of this cardinal earth sign are symbolized by the intriguing mer-goat–a combination of merman and goat. The creature uses its fishy tail to dive down to the bottom of the ocean of our collective consciousness where it collects a dream, which it takes to the top of the highest mountain, as nimble as a mountain goat.

## The mood under a Capricorn Moon

More dour, focused, and competent than before. The attitude on the street may be businesslike and a little humorless, but don't take that grimness personally. Politics simmer in the office and club; we get strategic and jostle for position. We may also think we know what everybody else should be doing. The Capricorn Moon supports our leadership qualities, but not everybody wants to be led.

We need to get work done, to see progress. It's important for us to have a list to check off for that sense of accomplishment. Mountain goats look pretty ordinary walking on flat terrain but are graceful athletes climbing up or down. Similarly, we can look ordinary and feel depressed without a mountain to climb.

## Romance

You can be right, or you can be happy. It's always good for a couple to have a project to work on together; it creates intimacy tangentially through collaboration. But you may need to remember that your goal is to weave togetherness rather than deciding whose methods are right. Work can interfere with a

romantic evening unless you incorporate it well. Each of you must be allowed to tell your own work story and feel supported by the other. Then you can focus on togetherness. Physical intimacy sparks, but not as easily as under other Moons, and an athletic quality may be needed to help us re-integrate our mind, heart, and body.

## Contemplation/meditation

Dive deep within and remember the loftiest dreams or ideals by which you guide your life. Hold that dream as a light at the top of the mountain and look at your life to see how your road has wound around the mountain, meandering through your days. Look upward. What steps do you need to take next to turn your path toward that mountaintop?

## Things to do

Think about your leadership. If we have a clear structure, we can mobilize our serious intent into productive action. Organize, make maps, work on schedules, outlines, make lists, set short-term goals to help achieve long-term goals. Empower others to do the same. Deal with bureaucrats, but be willing to humor them to smooth the way, because people can get very attached to their systems under a Capricorn Moon.

To get people into a better mood, ask about their personal projects or professional work and support their efforts. Report to the bosses and share your progress. Let them know that you've got everything under control. If you're having trouble, it's a great time to seek advice; people are free with information and unusually good at providing it sequentially. If you think someone else needs help, check to make sure it's not your anxiety speaking, and then offer what you know. But leave the person in control; we need to be the authors of our own life under this Moon.

## Garden

Graft or prune trees, train vines for strength and fruitfulness, plant root crops, harvest fruits and vegetables to be dried and stored long-term.

# What to watch out for

**Obstruction:** Don't get in other people's way. Support their work and help them to do whatever it is they are doing, or get out of the way.

**Depression:** Clear one drawer, take one thing off the list, make one call toward those long-term goals, and the depression usually eases.

**Anxiety:** We can get wound up if we feel out of control, or like we're not on schedule and in rhythm. If so, breathe deeply and set about solving one problem at a time.

**Controlling behavior:** Anxiety can turn into offering extraneous advice. The more anxious or concerned people are, the more controlling they can become. Boss or parent, lover or friend, policeman or politician, suddenly everybody seems to know what should be done and how.

**Being uptight:** We can have high expectations of ourselves and get wound just a little too tight, with our shoulders high and our teeth gritted. Consciously relax, stretch, find the humor in the situation, and feel your competence improve.

Navigate your day with . . .

# The Moon in Aquarius

The humanitarian interests of this fixed air sign are symbolized by a person pouring a pot of water onto dry land.

## The mood under an Aquarius Moon

Gather a team and get working together. The mood is social, political, tolerant, prudent, and experimental, but not particularly intimate. We want to understand the philosophy and theory behind an action before we agree to it. We can be farsighted about the big picture, but a little dense about the needs of those closest to us.

We notice how we can affect our community, family, and teams, and how these groups affect us. Meetings prosper if kept open-ended, because we can work unusually well in a group. We can stand back and be philosophical about our lives, achieve some distance and perspective about our emotional situations, but we can also be remarkably stubborn about our opinions and pet theories.

## Romance

Now is the time to enjoy the theory of romance. You can light the candles and put rose petals in the bathtub, but it may feel more like a delightful play than a moment of true intimacy. To get to know your beloved, spend time with his friends and ask big questions about his politics, spiritual path, or hopes and dreams for an ideal life. Think about it, share your own, and don't argue about who's right or wrong.

## Contemplation/meditation

You are a single cell in the body of the world. To be a healthy cell you must take care of your needs and live up to your potential. To be a healthy cell in the body of all beings, you need to know that you're doing your part and balancing your needs with the needs of others. Your suffering and joy are no more, or less, important than the suffering and joy of anyone else. Your job is to reduce the total suffering and increase the total joy of the whole body of all beings. But only you can find that balance.

## Things to do

While the mood is more collaborative and outgoing than under other Moons, we should reach out to new clients and delve into a new corner of the community. Take a yoga class. Have tea with coworkers. Deal with human resources. Hire a new member of the team and set about teambuilding exercises. Connect with your constituency. Pitch the boss a new idea. Campaign door-to-door. Have your gang over for drinks or dinner, or head to the bar for trivia night.

The Moon in Aquarius encourages us to live by our philosophy and so it's a good time to discuss politics, but people will listen more if we share our ideas rather than tell them they are wrong. While we can be unusually open-minded and curious about a fresh perspective, underneath the smile can be a steely intransigence.

## Garden

Don't plant, but help the constituents of the garden to work better together–cultivate, weed, curtail pests, and share the garden's bounty with neighbors.

# What to watch out for

**Disconnection:** The gift of objectivity can be used to disconnect us from our feelings or from the feelings of others. Keep a pathway between head, heart, and body open and flowing.

**Righteousness:** When we're right, we're right, or at least we think so. We can get caught up in our philosophy and preconceptions, feel we have the moral upper hand, and no one can budge us. If we feel ourselves getting up on a high horse, let's remember that this is a defense, and the cure is empathy.

**Contrariness:** Under the Aquarius Moon we can debate one side, then turn the tables around and debate the other. It's great to challenge other people's preconceptions as long as we're willing to challenge our own in the process.

**Farsightedness:** Sure we can see the big picture, but we can also miss the hurt feelings, needs, or excitement of the people closest to us.

**Being experimental:** This can be a gift or a problem. We can throw the baby out with the bathwater or want to try something new just because it's new. There's nothing wrong with that as long as we keep our eyes open to what really works in the long run.

Navigate your day with . . .

# The Moon in Pisces

Pisces is a mutable water sign. The ability to swim the archetypal lakes and streams of emotion and intuition is symbolized by two fish swimming in opposite directions.

## The mood under a Pisces Moon

This sensitive and permeable lunar mood can leave us feeling delicate, charming, empathic, vulnerable, teary, and easily tired. We reconnect with the backlog of intimacy, with feelings that may have been put on hold during the last few pragmatic Moons. Our intuition and imagination can overrule our logic and reason, our hearts can soften with compassion, but because we feel so much, we feel guilty easily and hate to have this quality abused. We can get sulky, unusually sensitive to criticism as well as to loud noise and the ugliness of the world. Concentration may be hard to hold as our imagination drifts in quickly. We soak up beauty, and the right music will feed our soul because our senses are heightened.

## Romance

Be tender and charming. Offer subtle romantic gestures, such as one lovely flower or a favorite food. Be aware of the energy between the two of you. Ask what he really needs that night, whether that's a long nap or a romantic night out, whatever nurtures mutual awareness and consideration. Speak up about what you need, and don't make him guess. Watch a soppy movie together, take in a gallery, or listen to music that moves your soul. Enjoy fine wine. Give each other a foot rub, since feet

can be unusually sensitive. Consideration and tenderness, and a moment of fantasy, help make it safe to keep the heart open.

## Contemplation/meditation

Imagine you are floating on a stormy sea. The waves are breaking around you but you are able to breathe. Allow yourself to drift below the storm into the calm of the deep ocean. Feel yourself supported and held in the water, this ocean connected through rivers and ponds to all the water on Earth, all flowing one into the other. Know this is a metaphor for our emotional milieu; our psyche floats in the great ocean. We are always affected by the feelings and experiences around us.

## Things to do

Find good uses for sensitivity and imagination. Meditate and pray. Dream up plans for the month ahead. Think about divination—use the tarot or I Ching, or scribe your crystal ball. Write down your dreams—they may be unusually informative. Do any form of subtle psychological or physical therapy. Finesse design. Experiment with appearance and environment and make subtle aesthetic decisions.

Go gently. Listen with all of your senses, because we send and receive messages on a very subtle level, whether or not we are conscious of them. And in the face of this sensitivity, learn to insulate, protect your energy fields out in public or with abrasive people. If others are unusually emotional, don't try to talk them out of it! And don't worry about fixing the situation. Rather than taking their feelings on, let them flow around you like a gentle stream.

## Garden

Under this fertile, moist, permeable Pisces Moon, set your plants in the ground, water and nurture them. Listen to them and find out what they need. Sing to them and imagine them growing strong. Both sides are unusually intuitive and open to one another.

# What to watch out for

**Self-pity:** Yes, it's time to acknowledge any backlog of emotion, both what hurt and what felt good. Sometimes we make the story worse in order to give ourselves permission to emote, and then wallow in self-pity, a highly disempowering experience. Be honest about your feelings and let them flow.

**Guilt trip:** It can be hard to ask directly for what we need. We may be tempted to make others feel guilty for our pain rather than take responsibility for our own self-care, but that backfires.

**Daydreaming:** We can consciously daydream an answer to our problems, but need to watch a tendency to drift into an escapist mindset and then realize we've wasted the day.

**Pain:** We're feeling unusually sensitive, so life can hurt, literally, unless we bring our attention to what feels right and what gives us faith that we're part of a beneficent world. It helps to be helpful to others.

**Allergies:** We may feel unusually permeable, so it pays to avoid things we know set off our allergies, as well as people whose behavior really makes us itch.

# Part III
# Phases and Aspects of the Moon

Now that you know what sign the Moon is shining through today or on the day you were born, the next step is to understand its strength and the quality of its energy through the phases of the Moon, as well as the flavor brought to it by the Moon's positional relationship to other planets, its aspects.

# Phases of the Moon and eclipses

Have you ever walked along a beach, watching the tide come in, and noticed the pounding urgency and enthusiasm as each wave surged higher up the shore? This is the feeling as the Moon waxes, or grows larger, in the night sky for two weeks from the New Moon until the Full Moon. We have wind in our sails, the energy builds, so ventures gather momentum easily.

As the Moon wanes, looks thinner, and grows darker each night for two weeks from the Full Moon to the New Moon, we integrate, put the pieces together, share what we know, and bring the work to completion.

The phase of the Moon describes this quality of energy, whether momentum-building or receding, created by the relationship (or aspect) between the Sun and the Moon. This cycle is fine-tuned to help us understand the energetic weather of the moment, and thus choose the best possible timing for any undertaking. The circuit is divided into eight distinct Moon phases, each with its own flavor and gift, and each about three-and-a-half days in duration.

First, let's play with the symbolism here. The phases of the Moon express the aspects, or relationship, between the Sun and the Moon, and describe how these two are coordinating or clashing in their call to us.

The Sun symbolizes the conscious world, what we see when the lights are on and the Sun is shining, what we agree is concrete reality. It signifies our life force, ego, and persona. The Sun sign of our birth speaks of our basic vitality, our consciousness, and mode of being. All the rest of the planets reflect the Sun's light.

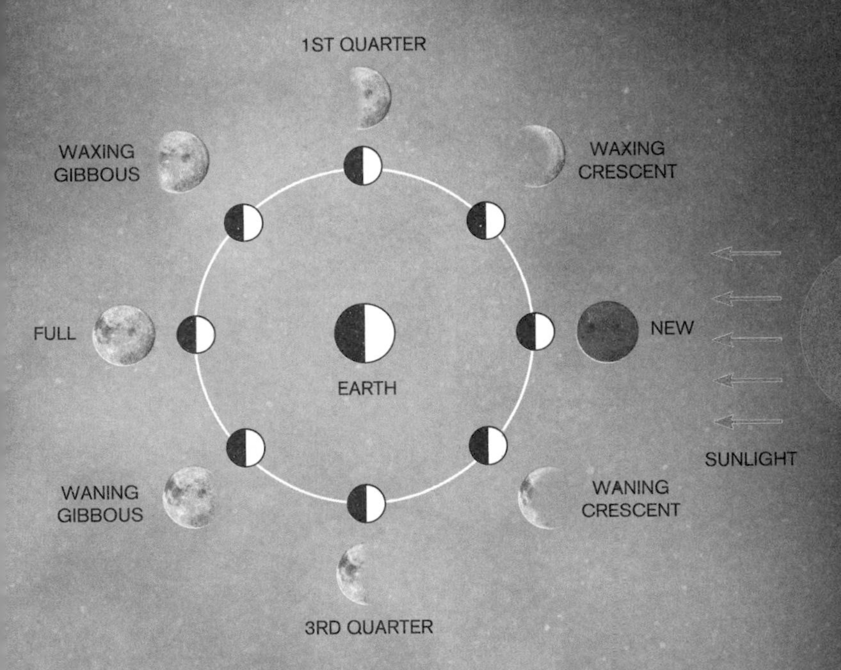


The Moon symbolizes our inner world, what happens in the dark, the unconscious, the hidden, and the habitual. In our personal charts, it describes our innermost emotions and how we express them, what inspires and incentivizes us, and how we look after and nourish ourselves and others.

In this section, first we look at the Moon cycle by person—how you express the Moon phase of your birth—and then we look at Moon phases by the day and eclipses.

# Moon phases by person

So how do you embody and express your Moon phase? The Moon phase of your birth helps you to understand where you are in a soul cycle. If you're born at the end of the cycle, that doesn't necessarily mean you're an old soul about to be enlightened, but it does mean you're completing a soul cycle.

**New Moon** If you were born just after the New Moon, it doesn't mean you're a young soul, but that you are starting off on a new soul project and are sailing into a life of discovery. Your feelings and actions work together, for better or worse. You're here in this life to explore and experiment, to find what excites you. When you're young, you can be open and enthusiastic, if a bit simplistic, and see events from a single perspective. You catch fire when you start a project and inspire others easily, but you might find it harder to maintain your enthusiasm and finish. After an adventurous and exploratory youth and early adulthood, you are able to find one thing you love, or are skilled at, and run with it. As you age, you learn to see layers of complexity and shades of gray, and finish what you begin.

**Waxing Crescent Moon** If you were born under the waxing Crescent Moon, you carry an inherent enthusiasm for life. The people who raised you probably trained you in different skills, which, while it may have created some confusion within you, gave you a versatile approach to the world. You can see both the gift of tradition and the need to innovate. On a bad day this may just leave you perplexed and conflicted, but on a good day it creates a solid but innovative person, balanced in tradition with an exploratory edge. Your inner versatility may lead you to wander over many paths and through diverse interests until you find the road that all parts of you agree upon.

**Waxing Half-Moon** You like a challenge but may have experienced more than you bargained for already this lifetime. You've wrestled with inner differences and built determination through overcoming obstacles. The adults who raised you may have been quite different from each other and expressed varying opinions, and you had to adjust and adapt in between. You can talk to anybody when you are feeling sociable because of this, or debate any comment when feeling contrary. It's easy for you to see interactions in terms of conflict, which in your midlife can make you a fierce advocate or competitor, builder, or problem solver. As you mature, you can learn to synthesize different opinions and create a framework for your unique approach.

**Waxing Gibbous Moon** The waxing Gibbous Moon brings an extra level of empathy to your chart. It can take the edge off a hard chart and soften an already sensitive one. You have had to juggle disparate personalities, which has given you versatility and flexibility in relationships. You can work for a cause you believe in, but can get anxious around more personal conflict, and tou may prefer not to fight. Your discomfort with the world as it is can encourage you to improve your environment and make the world a better place. Your early years can take you on a journey through several different chapters where you acquire a variety of skills. You may be more comfortable finding your own path and working for yourself than balancing personalities in a large organization. These many different threads begin to synthesize into one picture in midlife and you see what you've been training for. As you age, you are rarely bored, and you continue to learn late into life.

**Full Moon** Born with the Sun and Moon opposite, you often tune in to the oppositions in your family and feel more comfortable with one or other parent in the room rather than both at the same time. You can love a variety of people with conflicting ideas, although may also prefer to be with them one at a time. A person willing to tackle the issues of our time, you can handle conflict head-on and be a fierce debater or advocate for the underdog, but you might squirm when you're in the room with other people fighting. You may have a strong emotional charge and come into relationships with personal baggage. Your hopes and fears need to be unpacked to make room for the relationship you really want. In your early teenage years you end one cycle and begin a new one, and you really get a chance to find yourself in your 30s and 40s. Work on respecting the different needs within you; help your mind and emotions to respect one another.

**Disseminating Gibbous Moon** You arrived in this life with a certain maturity of soul and whispers of a calling. Your childhood may have been full of odd stories that felt important but didn't quite make sense, as if you were reading the last chapter in a long novel, but never saw the first part. Your early life may feel like a review session, reminding you of what you already know. Adulthood is probably more comfortable. You need a life with variety, but not everything interests you. You understand the world as a truly complex place and can sometimes feel overwhelmed or discouraged. If so, bring your focus in, come back to what you know and love to renew, and then return to your busy life. Over time, your ability to share what you know increases, so you can teach, speak about, and train what you've come to understand.

**Waning Half-Moon** You may have been around some rip-roaring debates, or perhaps your childhood involved someone who felt at odds with the world. When you dig your heels in, no one can budge you. You question the status quo and know it can be better. The first seven years or so of your life may have been uncomfortably eventful and given you a lot to think about, giving rise to your compassion. You have a knack for spotting a problem and can help people resolve conflicts. You may feel like you really arrived in this lifetime in your adolescence and enjoy your growing wisdom as an older person.

**Balsamic Crescent Moon** You came here to complete a project. You're probably very good at what you're good at and totally apathetic about what you're not interested in. You may have precocious skills or known early on what would become your focus of interest. You may carry a strong sense of responsibility for a few key people in your life. As a child, you may have been mistaken for being older than you were, and people generally think you know what you're talking about. But if you need a hug, or need help, you have to ask. Later in your life you may feel like you're starting anew, diversifying, and setting the seeds for the next chapter.

# Moon phases by the day

The cycle begins at the New Moon. Roughly every 28 days a new lunar cycle begins when the Moon is dark, invisible to us (but powerful within us), because it is positioned in front of the Sun and shines all the light back toward the Sun. Our symbols of consciousness (Sun) and unconsciousness (Moon), outer structure (Sun) and inner feelings (Moon) align or conjunct. Our dreams and emotions activate and initiate a new cycle.

The farther the Moon moves away from the Sun in its circle around the Earth, the more light we see reflected. Our night sky, symbolic of our inner world, our subconscious realm, becomes illuminated. Use the lunar energy of the waxing Moon to begin, initiate, plant, increase growth, gain, attract. The wind is in the sails and we can launch a journey. After the Full Moon, as the now waning Moon circles back toward the Sun, it reflects less, and the night grows darker. Instead of instigating new projects, this is a time to integrate, prune, review, complete, amalgamate, sort, come to understand, and teach what we learned.

## New Moon

### 0–3½ days after the New Moon

### Sun and Moon conjunct

Around the time of the New Moon, check in with your feelings, hunches, and goals. Listen to your nighttime dreams and daydreaming meanderings for clues about this next cycle. The Sun and Moon are now in the same sign, sending you the same signals and instructions–listen and step forward. Initiate a new path. Start a project. Reach out.

Traditionally, this is a time to do a simple Moon ritual. Think about what you want to accomplish on a practical, emotional, or spiritual level this month. Write or speak that intention clearly, and take action in that direction. It can be as magical as lighting a candle and calling on your guides and angels to help manifest, or an informal, sociable ritual, a chance to sit with your circle of friends to share intentions for the month and toast them with wine. It can be as pragmatic as stating your intention and then doing three practical things toward achieving it, such as making a phone call, setting up a file, and locating a resource. Watch the magic build when you do all three—meditate, share, and act.

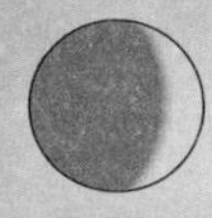

## Waxing Crescent Moon
### 3½–7 days after the New Moon
### Sun and Moon semi-square

Here comes a splash of reality. Notice the glitches, problems, and differences of opinion. Kids grow restless. Writers can hit a snag or writer's block. Boredom or anxiety can arise if we feel overwhelmed by options or realize that what we've just begun may take some work. We can become impatient or feel inconvenienced and react as small setbacks irritate our old patterns. But a little sweat equity goes a long way now, so keep circling back to the projects you care about and take them a step further. Be patient with ego issues (they will arise), and let differing viewpoints fertilize the conversation. We can feel unsettled, but use this quality to experiment, consider options, and brainstorm ideas.

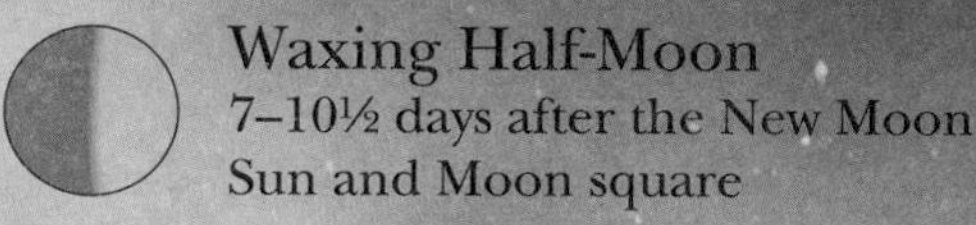

## Waxing Half-Moon

### 7–10½ days after the New Moon

### Sun and Moon square

People tend to square off as the Sun and Moon move into a right angle. Our head and heart may disagree. Clothes may feel too tight or uncomfortable. The mood can be argumentative, but also productive and realistic. We may have a crisis. The conflicts of desire may be between ourselves and others or between competing needs within ourselves. Our ideas can come in at right angles. Like cars at a crossroads, we need a good system so they don't collide. Differing viewpoints can give us a more realistic understanding of our situation. Our challenge is to see both sides and find a third alternative that works for all.

We can put this difficult, conflict-oriented energy to good use. Be courageous. Tackle a person, problem, or pile in the closet that needs extra bravery. Engage in sports or a physical workout and compete with your personal best. Avoid a tendency to frame every conversation as conflict; practice diplomacy instead. But if you need to invoke a healthy confrontation, this is a good time to do so.

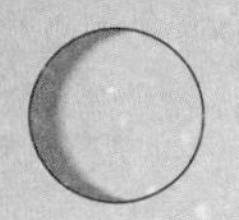

## Waxing Gibbous Moon

### 10½–14 days after the New Moon

### Sun and Moon sesqui-quadrate

The energy swells, momentum builds, but we can be distracted or feel our attention stretched thin by a suddenly busy schedule. Maybe we do need to diversify, to round our life out and not just focus on one thing at a time. Our work will go faster if we take a break and respond to the extraneous needs that seem to interrupt our schedule. Our time with friends or coworkers will go more smoothly if we listen to their perspective, even though it may seem inconsequential or off mark to us. Honor these distracting voices, but stay in there and shepherd important projects through. It's a good time to seek a second opinion. It's also an excellent time to choose a bunch of contrasting colors to light up a room or present our counterpoint to light up a project.

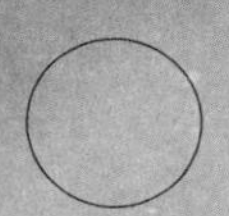

## Full Moon

### 14–17½ days after the New Moon

### Sun and Moon opposition

The Full Moon brings a culmination of energy and celebrates a high tide. Emotions are running high and our subconscious can run the show. If we've been acknowledging and integrating our feelings all month long, we'll get a swell of harmonious energy but no big surprises. If we've been suppressing how we feel or not honoring our inner nature, that awareness can rip through us now. With this extra swell of emotional energy, it's a powerful time to perform or make a presentation that really grabs our hearts. It can be a dramatic, tricky but successful time to make a statement or go to court because we move into adversarial positions so easily. For the same reason, it's not a good time for a wedding or to sign a business partnership.

To take care of ourselves under the Full Moon, we should acknowledge inconvenient feelings or ideas. What part of us now needs to be expressed? Do we need to dance the night away or sing in the shower? Go for it. But if we're really ticked off at work, let's tell our journal or a friend what we'd really like to say to the boss, but wait a few days to consider and act wisely on this impulse. Acknowledge feelings and they won't just rip out and create surprises.

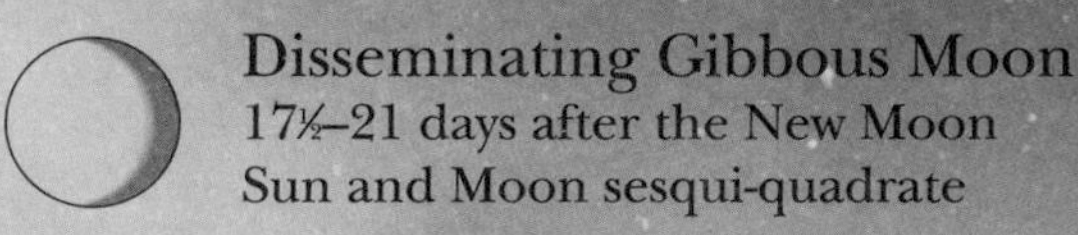

## Disseminating Gibbous Moon

17½–21 days after the New Moon
Sun and Moon sesqui-quadrate

Tensions soften, but again we're distracted. Kids, friends, dogs can clamor for attention and remind us to keep our lives whole and balanced. We may notice a let-down in energy, as if we were crashing from too many espressos. Our bodies may feel stressed and appreciate a hot bath or massage. Our crops are ripening, and we begin to see the result of our efforts in this month's cycle, the product of both our intention and whatever other agenda the universe had waiting for us. We are also reminded of ongoing responsibilities that we may have ignored recently. Consciously follow on the main projects and assume the distractions or irritations have a purpose. They're here to stretch us, train us, and help us sort irrelevant distractions from important side lessons.

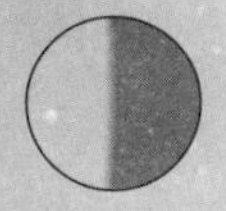

## Waning Half-Moon

21–24½ days after the New Moon
Sun and Moon square

Assess. Three-quarters of the way through this lunar cycle we should be able to see pretty much what's working and what's not. We can also see clearly what we agree with and what we don't. We may feel contentious or need to confront a problem, but can do so with more reason and forethought than in the first quarter. Learn from discomfort and become conscious of where to keep up the work. This is a good time to take a test or notice that you are being tested. But, like a martial arts test at a dojo, the teacher thinks you can win this one. Productive discontent can help us finish, polish, reassess, make corrections.

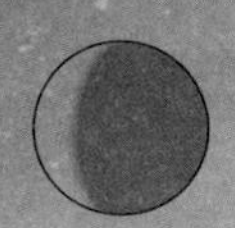

## Balsamic Crescent Moon

24½–28 days after the New Moon

Sun and Moon semi-square

As the Moon enters its dark phase, our inner mood quietens down and we clarify our understanding. It's time to sort the seeds of the last lunar cycle. Our physical energy may be low, but this calm allows us to see deep within. Our memories walk with us. This quiet in-breath encourages introspection, meditation, therapeutic conversation, scrying, and divination, as well as finding and addressing root causes. Take a moment to look back over the last month and assess life. Listen to dreams. Come to stillness, if only for a moment. Prepare for the next cycle.

# Eclipses

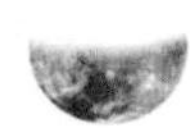

Think of an eclipse as a form of astrological acupuncture that can unblock energy flow and precipitate events that were already ripening. A super-focused New Moon or Full Moon concentrate their energy like a laser beam, and when an eclipse hits close to an important place in our personal chart, what was stuck becomes unstuck. Opportunities arise, although we may swear at the time. An element of our life, whether a person, thing, or idea, may be eclipsed and we have to let go. Like deadwood pruned from a tree, this creates room for new growth. The changes nudged along by an eclipse can be surprising, often uncomfortable, yet sometimes wonderful. In retrospect, we can usually see how important or inevitable these changes were.

## A solar eclipse (super New Moon)

This is a potent and directed force. If a solar eclipse occurs in the same sign as your Sun, Moon, or other planets, you may get an opportunity to start a new cycle that brings fresh honesty and integrity to your situation, whether you like it or not.

**Example of a classic solar eclipse event:** Evelyn hated her insurance job but felt she had to stay for security's sake. As a solar eclipse approached her Moon, she accidentally forwarded a cartoon critical of the boss, to her boss. With a twitch of her finger she lost her job, gave up a dead-end illusion of security, and created the room to go back to school to pursue veterinary medicine, her heart's real desire.

## A lunar eclipse (super Full Moon)

The volume is turned up so we understand what we really feel and need. We can't just stuff these needs and feelings under

the carpet when a lunar eclipse dances on our chart. We have to get real and deal with it.

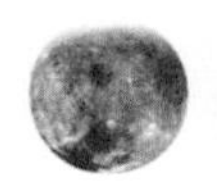

**Example of a classic lunar eclipse event:** Fred couldn't stand his in-laws and dealt with this by avoiding them at all costs. He'd rather work than vacation with his wife in her parents' mountain cabin. One year he agreed to fetch her and at the same time observe the lunar eclipse (coincidently near his Mars). He drove up into the mountains but an unexpected storm rolled in and he was snowed in with his in-laws for three days. They argued, let it go, survived, got to know one another, and began to build some trust, although they never did vacation together.

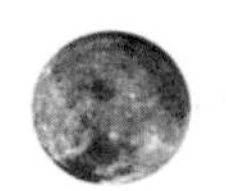

## The mechanics of an eclipse

The Moon usually appears a little north or south of the Sun's orbit because the plane of its orbit is tilted compared with the Earth's plane. The points where these two planes meet are called the lunar nodes. Twice a year, the Sun, Moon, and Earth align along the lunar nodes in such a straight line that the New Moon covers the face of the Sun and we have an eclipse. At the Full Moon, before or after the solar eclipse, the Earth's shadow covers the Moon and we have a lunar eclipse.

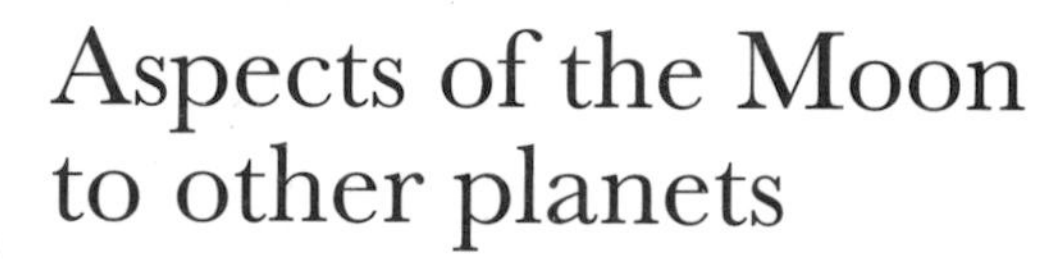

# Aspects of the Moon to other planets

The planets form relationships, or geometric patterns known as aspects, with the Moon and flavor its energy, like adding basil and garlic to soup. Our daily emotional milieu, the vibrational soup in which we swim, is created by the sign of the Moon, the phase of the Moon, and the next planet to which the Moon relates. The Moon is almost always in relationship to a planet. When it finishes with one aspect, it reaches out to the next, like a square dancer handing off from one partner to the next as he/she moves around the circle.

In common with all relationships, some are easier than others. Easy or supportive aspects, such as conjunction, trine, or sextile, suggest an opportunity. When the Moon makes a challenging aspect, such as square or opposition, the mood can be more abrasive or uncomfortable. Yet, if we work with it, this discomfort can inspire positive action.

**Easier aspects:** Conjunction (together), trine (one third of the way around the zodiac), and sextile (half a trine, or one sixth of the way around the circle) describe an easy, supportive flow between the energies of the two planets. Think of these aspects like running into an old friend–comfortable, supportive, and cooperative.

**Challenging aspects:** Square (one-fourth of the way around the zodiac) and opposition (directly across from one another, like the Sun and Moon at a Full Moon) are tension-producing and discordant. Semi-square (45 degrees apart, or half a square) and sesqui-quadrate (135 degrees apart) are irritating. Sometimes a challenge is good for us, though, and gets us motivated. Think of a tough teacher or high-maintenance

partner—the relationship may not be easy, but it can teach us or call on us to grow to meet the challenge.

## How to use aspects

First, go to an astrological calendar—see appendix (page 150)—or search online for "astrological Moon aspects for the day."

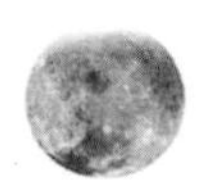

**Astrological weather** Once we know the Moon's sign and phase, establishing which planets are relating to the Moon puts us in touch with the flavor of the day, so we can work with mood.

**Example:** If you know that today Mars forms a tough aspect to the Moon in Scorpio, you see that the rather cynical Scorpio Moon mood is made even more irascible with a square from Mars. You don't need to take personally the snarky comments from coworkers, you aren't surprised by rudeness on the subway home, and you may reschedule that dinner with your in-laws.

**Example:** On Monday you have a big promotional meeting, a therapy appointment in the afternoon, and a hot date planned afterward. Go to your astrological calendar or website, find the sign of the Moon and the major Moon aspects that day. That will help you to build a picture of the interpersonal weather and relate it to the events of the day. See if it matches your plans, or take the cues to prepare or adjust your plans to make the most of the day.

**Planning** If we want to choose a good time for an event, it's helpful to have the Moon in supportive relationship to a planet that is helpful to our goals. If we're scheduling a planning meeting, for example, we can look for a good relationship between the Moon and Mercury. For romance at an art opening,

we can choose a day when the Moon is flavored by a trine from Venus. We can use the Moon's aspects to help with timing events large or small.

**Weddings:** Choose a wedding date that has a waxing Moon in an earth or water sign with supportive aspects from Venus or Jupiter. Avoid a Full Moon or Moon in a challenging aspect to Uranus or Pluto. If the wedding is for an older couple, the phase and sign of the Moon are less important, but look for those harmonious aspects.

**Starting a business:** Launch on a date that has a waxing Moon with supportive aspects to Saturn and planets that fit the business. Choose fire-sign or air-sign Moons for public businesses, an earth-sign Moon for more pragmatic construction, and a water-sign Moon for healing practices.

**Asking for a raise:** Pick a day that has a waxing Moon in fire or air signs with positive aspects to Venus and Jupiter.

**Planning a party:** Look for a Moon in an ebullient, outgoing fire or air sign, with the Moon in positive relationship to Venus, Jupiter, Uranus, or Mars. Avoid a Moon in challenging aspects to Saturn or Pluto.

**Planning surgery:** Look for a Moon in the first or last quarter in supportive relationship to Mercury, Mars, or any relationship to Saturn. For optional surgery, avoid the Full Moon.

**Confronting an opponent:** Do it on a day that has a balanced Moon. Aspects that give you courage also give your opponent strength. Look for positive aspects to Saturn for clear boundaries, Mars for courage and assertiveness, and Mercury for eloquence.

**Cutting hair to grow better:** Go for a waning Moon in fire or air signs with good aspects to Venus.

**Cutting hair to stay short:** Choose a Moon in earth or water signs with good aspects to Venus.

**Planting seeds:** Ideally, choose a waxing Moon in Taurus, Cancer, or Pisces. Avoid challenging aspects to Saturn and Pluto.

**Arranging a family meeting:** Look for a Gemini, Libra, or Aquarius Moon with supportive aspects to Mercury, Jupiter, or Venus. If the meeting is to build new systems or structures, see if you can get Saturn in the mix.

## Void-of-course Moon

Once the Moon has made its last aspect and has no more conversation or relationship with another planet until it changes sign, it is considered to be void of course. Then the rhythm of our daily life goes out of sync, as if the car we're driving goes into neutral. It's a wonderful time to sit still, meander through a museum, or engage in any internal or subjective experience. It's not a great time to make decisions or launch projects, because decisions may be unrealistic and projects have trouble coming to completion. Meetings held under a void-of-course Moon tend to meander and wander indecisively.

You can easily work through this, but it may take conscious effort. If you have to make a decision or major purchase under a void-of-course Moon, do it with care and persistence, and keep the receipt. If you are in a meeting that begins to wander off course, come back to your agenda and help people to stay on track.

# Aspects of the Moon by person

You imprinted the qualities of the Moon at the moment of your birth. The planet in relationship to the Moon at that moment colors your emotional nature, your experience of nurturing and of the women around you, and flavors what makes you feel at home for the rest of your life.

Easy or supportive relationships, such as conjunction, trine, or sextile, suggest an easy collaboration between your emotional nature and that planet. When the Moon makes a challenging relationship, such as square or opposition, the relationship between your emotional nature and that planet is more abrasive, like a teacher who challenges you to make you learn. Yet, if you work with it, uncomfortable aspects often are the greatest source of success, because they push you to grow and achieve.

Yes, there are subtleties between the various supportive and challenging aspects that are worth investigating with an astrologer, but we make a good start here.

# The Moon and … Mercury

**If the Moon was in a supporting aspect to Mercury at your birth,** your mind and heart work together. They bring mental agility, give you a special charismatic touch, and help you to find the right words to reach the public. You can be clever, witty, often charming and creative, and can excel at any job where you need to think fast and respond on the spot. But if you don't want to be just glib, you have to choose to look deeply. You learn quickly and may pass multiple-choice tests with ease, but need to study in-depth if you actually want the information.

**If the Moon was in a challenging aspect to Mercury at your birth,** You have mental agility, even brilliance, but these aspects can make your learning process a little peculiar. You have to find the learning style that works for you. You can get anxious or worried if you focus on what could go wrong without considering what could go right. Sometimes your mind doesn't know how to shut off and keeps the brain's hamster-wheel going all night unless you find ways to relax. You can communicate eloquently but sometimes feel it is so important to be heard that you become impatient with the process of dialog. This improves with age.

If you feel nervous or torn between an emotional and logical response, let your heart and mind have a good talk with one another. Pretend they sit on either side of the room and speak from your mind to your heart, then from heart to mind, and mediate dialog between them. On a more pragmatic level, meditation or games of mental focus can help, as does any exercise to lower your stress level and realign your nervous system. Acupuncture, yoga, all efforts at stress relief will help you tap into your scintillating potential.

# The Moon and … Venus

**If the Moon was in a supporting aspect to Venus at your birth,** you are infused with grace and charm and can soften many otherwise hard aspects of the chart. Beauty is not optional for you. Although Venus has generally expensive tastes, it really is more about the aesthetics than the cost. You can create beauty wherever you go. People like you and tend to give you things, so this aspect adds luck. Your hopes, fears, and excitement about relationships can take up a large part of your emotional landscape. You network easily, because you understand the nature of connections, and people tend to remember you. You have a seductive quality, so use your powers for good.

**If the Moon was in a challenging aspect to Venus at your birth,** you have charm with attitude. People may be drawn to you, but you may have little respect for social niceties. Own up to the fact that you're more social than you admit, but are not really secure in your lovability. You'd prefer others to make the first overture and so make connection safe for you. Really, you feel for others and don't want to hurt anyone, but sometimes your self-protection does just that. The more you own your warmth and kindness, the more comfortable you become in social situations, and the more beautiful.

You may be tempted by retail therapy. Beauty feeds you and nurtures you, but consider creating it yourself rather than buying it, because if you keep importing it, not only will you be broke, you may never quite feed the hunger. So when your heart feels like it's on hot coals, create beauty by expressing affection–be kind to a neighbor, or chat to someone who could use your special brand of warmth and your own heart will calm down.

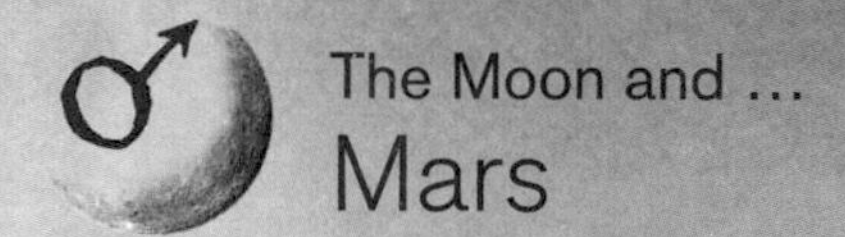

# The Moon and … Mars

**If the Moon was in a supporting aspect to Mars at your birth,** power is added to your mood and assertiveness to your demeanor. You probably had some muscle-building experiences as a kid and had to roll with conflict or manage strong personalities that taught you to stand up for yourself. You are familiar and comfortable with strong women. Often you see what needs to be done and have the energy to get the ball rolling. Engage your ability to be an advocate for the weak. Just watch a tendency to run roughshod over less assertive types.

**If the Moon was in a challenging aspect to Mars at your birth,** a strong, inner combustion engine drives you to get things done. You may have had a powerful adolescence, but taken time to recalibrate as an adult. Sometimes you order other people around–a leftover from adapting to willful personalities as a kid. In a job requiring firm leadership this is wonderful, but it may need to be dialed back in a relationship. Your inner adolescent is enthusiastic but always ready to get pugnacious. You probably came by your defensiveness with good cause, but now you have to ask yourself if it will still serve you. If you can channel your inner fire into action and not reaction, you will go far.

If you find yourself angry, irritable, or accident-prone, find a good outlet for your physical energy, such as athletics, dance, or martial arts, so it doesn't swirl into tension or temper. Then find a way to develop your role as guardian, the positive refrain for militancy. It's easy to do this in the military or police, but you can also use this guardian capacity to protect family, business, or health, or be a champion for a worthy cause. Just make sure those people want to be guarded.

## 24 The Moon and ...
# Jupiter

**If the Moon was in a supporting aspect to Jupiter at your birth**, you are imbued with a philosophical perspective and a general philanthropic desire to see the good in people–to believe if we just keep the conversation going, we can get to the bottom of things. Publicity and respect come easily to you. You may not always respect boundaries and may be surprised when other people don't share your magnanimous views. Your approach is so natural to you that you have trouble understanding people who take moral shortcuts or get bitter instead of active. But you can help other people see the good in themselves and help us all find the silver lining.

**If the Moon was in a challenging aspect to Jupiter at your birth**, you keep the charm, luck, natural sense of bounty, and optimism, which can soften harder aspects in your chart, but you need to watch a tendency to overdo or to be overtrusting. You can overdo worry, excitement, concern, any emotional extreme, but have the ability to bounce back. This Moon sings "Don't worry, be happy." Keep that optimism but also keep your eyes open.

If you feel that you are overindulging or giving too much and no one else is giving back, ask if you can give yourself the gift of balance instead.

ħ

# The Moon and …
# Saturn

**If the Moon was in a supporting aspect to Saturn at your birth,** it may have brought you maturity at an early age. One of your parents may have had to play both roles, which left you feeling as though you had to take the world seriously and develop competence early. Learning how to play is your next challenge. You may be wary of taking on responsibility, or of getting too close to anybody because you consider this a responsibility, and you take your responsibilities seriously. You have a craftsman's talent and stick to what you begin. You do your homework, apprentice well, and learn by doing. Your home may be more organized than cozy, but that works for you.

**If the Moon was in a challenging aspect to Saturn at your birth,** seriously motivating aspects spur you on. Although depression whispers to you whenever you hold still for too long, you have the ambition and drive to accomplish most things. You can be competent and resolute, but driven by a haunting concern that what you do and who you are is not enough. Other people don't see this; they just see your accomplishments. If you get depressed and decide to be miserable, you do that with equal success. It's up to you. After learning through challenges, you grow into a rich and active maturity. It can be hard for you to mother yourself or others; you may not have had much cuddling as a child. Learn to nurture yourself the way you wish you had been nurtured and your competence will have more fuel.

When your world seems to be out of control or you feel too driven to relax, make self-care your goal. You can control your actions and choose to be ambitious about health, calmness, joy, and contentment.

# The Moon and … Uranus

**If the Moon was in a supporting aspect to Uranus at your birth,** brilliance, humor, nervous energy, and lateral-thinking ability are yours. As a matter of fact, it may be hard for you to think conventionally. Naturally inventive, you may have trouble learning the ordinary steps or following usual etiquette. Your upbringing had an eccentric edge that has helped you to adapt and think for yourself. You may be more at home with technology than some. Slowing down your nervous system to connect with others may be a bit of a challenge. Have patience and allow for people working at a different rhythm.

**If the Moon was in a challenging aspect to Uranus at your birth,** you have brilliance still, but you need to add control. Impulse control may be an abstract concept for you. You can react so fast that other people don't feel you've listened carefully to them. You can jump to conclusions and sound arrogant. Your security and comfort may have been interrupted by unexpected events as a child, so you're good at handling what life throws at you, but can be anxious when things get boring and stable. You're naturally inventive but can be eternally restless, looking for greener pastures or trying to improve the situation. If you can direct this discontent toward work, it's easier for you to build more contentment at home.

Work with your nervous system when you feel nervous or discontent. Use meditation, Tai Chi, Reiki, any of the healing arts that help direct nervous energy so it works for you and not against you. When you're in a situation that you can't change, think about what you can change. Find allies who see that change is necessary, and put your energy there.

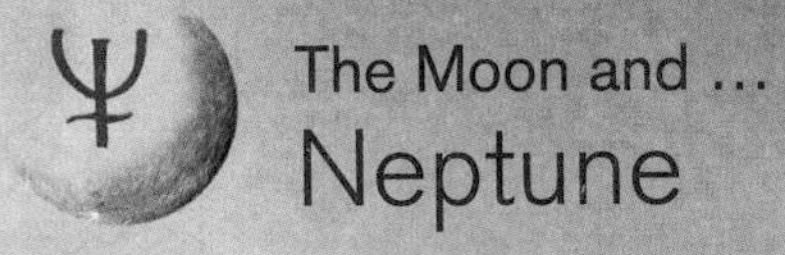

# The Moon and … Neptune

**If the Moon was in a supporting aspect to Neptune at your birth,** your personality has a certain creative mystique. You can be an intuitive sponge, so learn where your feelings begin and theirs end. You may have trouble setting boundaries with your mother and other women in your life, but appreciate a strong intuitive connection with your beloveds. Harsh sounds and ugly sights grate on your nerves, whereas music feeds your soul. Like a chameleon, if you don't like how you feel, you change your environment and your mood. It soothes you to be in a community that agrees with your metaphysical understanding.

**If the Moon was in a challenging aspect to Neptune at your birth,** reality can be a bit difficult. You may come from a long line of intuitive women and be a natural on the inner realms but have to live in the practical modern world. Since you pick up so much from your environment, you can easily feel overwhelmed. You need time out but have to watch that escapist streak. Learn to tell the difference between your imagination and your active intuition–they can jumble up within.

In the face of feeling overwhelmed or lost, it helps to take a two-pronged approach. First, honor your Neptune and create an altar or prayer space, or a place where you can dive into your creative work. Alternatively, take yourself away from all this with a good bath and a good book. Do not be tempted by drugs or alcohol because you may be unusually susceptible, and they will make your reality harder to return to. For the second prong, imagine a life that would be wonderful enough to stay present and grounded within, and then begin to make it so.

## The Moon and ...
# Pluto

**If the Moon was in a supporting aspect to Pluto at your birth**, you may have earned the extra depth this combination provides by being there for yourself in your childhood through lonely times when parents or carers were distracted or difficult. You can help others to explore their soul because you've searched your own. If there's a problem, you want to look it squarely in the face, which gives you a special talent for work where depth and presence are required. Your feelings run deep, and you can appear reserved. You're there for your friends in tough times, but may be a little bored by them on a good day. Small talk leaves you cold, but let someone begin to share his/her real story, and you're right there.

**If the Moon was in a challenging aspect to Pluto at your birth**, there's not much you can't handle, because there's not much you haven't handled. However, you may have no patience with the mundane world. You may have a slightly morbid streak that makes you curious about dire events, but this is part of your training to cope. An obsessive-compulsive streak can kick in when you're emotional but don't have clear direction. You can be volcanic or implode when angry and are particularly triggered by issues of abuse and oppression. If friends tell you to lighten up, they don't understand your gift. Paradoxically, you may calm down when working on the front lines or tackling real problems.

To counteract this tension, explore the depths. Therapy can be fascinating as a way of developing new understanding. Undertake a radical act of compassion, too–if your heart hurts, find a friend who is sadder than you are and listen to his/her woes. It helps to tap into a real need and find a way of helping.

# The Moon's planetary aspects by day

If we look at mythology from around the globe, the stories about the planets' persona may be very different, but the characteristics of those personalities are amazingly similar, no matter whose mythology we examine.

Astrologers usually refer to Roman mythology because it's so familiar and easily available. Anything you remember about gods and goddesses will help you to understand the symbolism of the planets. The Roman archetypes had their special gifts to bestow, and a part of the real world to oversee, and often got themselves into deep trouble. The goddess Venus was a sucker for a compliment, and loyalty wasn't her forte. Mars fought about anything and everything. Mercury was brilliant, but not always honest. Correspondingly, each planet represents a spectrum from a problematic side through practical matters to divinely bestowed gifts.

Some planets, such as Saturn and Pluto, have a more obvious malefic or challenging side. Others, such as Venus and Jupiter, have a more obviously beneficent side, but all contain this spectrum. We don't get to choose which planet is affecting us, but we do get to choose which end of the spectrum we live out.

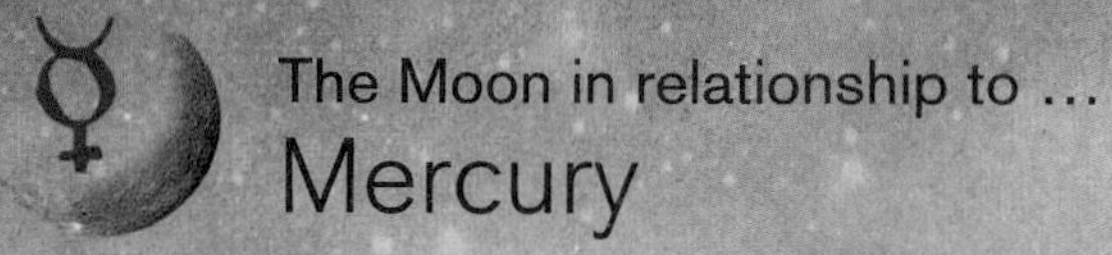

# The Moon in relationship to ... Mercury

Do you need to think, talk, travel? Choose a good relationship between the Moon and Mercury. The messenger, patron saint of the modern world, describes our mental switchboard–how we move, talk, and organize our thinking. Practical Mercury also controls the traffic of our life and is expressed through all systems and methods that help people, things, ideas, and information get around–the Internet, tablets, phones, newspapers, broadcasting, airplanes, cars, trains, and simple conversations.

**If the Moon is in a supporting aspect to Mercury**, speed and consciousness are increased, as are the ability to think things through and find perspective. We may bring our minds to any problem and find an answer. This side of the Moon in Mercury supports swift movement, understanding, divine wisdom, intellect, introspection, adjustment, ease in communication, promotion and broadcasting, travel, nervous systems, and electronic systems.

**If the Moon is in a challenging aspect to Mercury**, a tendency to get lost in the mind inspires glitches in all things. We can get more edgy, irritable, anxious, scattered, diffused, glib, and have to deal with theft, dishonesty, rationalization, or an argument between head and heart.

Use the positive expression of Mercury to solve the problem. Reconnect your mind and your heart. Attend to your nervous system, take a deep breath, and relax. Get your companions to talk, and listen to them. It doesn't matter so much what they say as long as they feel heard.

## The moon in relationship to … Venus

Do you need to be diplomatic, affectionate, show great taste, develop self-worth, nurture romance, get married? Choose a good relationship between the Moon and Venus. Venus, gracious muse and queen of matters of the heart and art, symbolizes our creative process, what we love, what we find beautiful and delicious, and what we value.

**If the Moon is in a supporting aspect to Venus**, sociability and compassion are boosted. These heart-warming aspects of the Moon in Venus soften us, lend us charm, and encourage diplomacy and kindness. They help any work or social situation where we need to inspire the goodwill of others. They also support the rights and care of women and help us to connect with our senses, so we feel affectionate and sensual. When the Moon relates to Venus, we are encouraged to build and buy beautiful things and to choose the right look or style for our hair.

**If the Moon is in a challenging aspect to Venus**, our social interactions may be nudged out of sync. These aspects may put us on edge, bring awkwardness and antisocial moments. Our hearts either cool off and stand back, or heat up with a longing for an unrequited love or expensive pair of shoes.

If your heart is stirred up, perform a random act of kindness, dig out the art supplies, or sing in the shower. Give those emotions somewhere productive to go. If you are in a delicate social situation, haul out a more formal Venus and be diplomatic and polite, even when feeling uncomfortable. Trust Venus to smooth over rough edges.

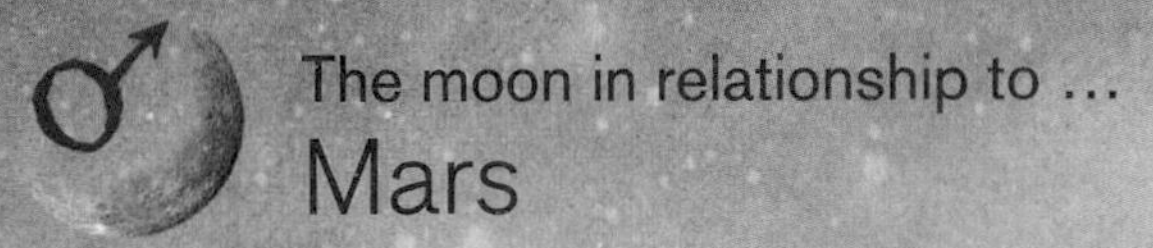

The moon in relationship to …

# Mars

Do you need to work out, take a stand, build a wall, win a contest, get physical? Look for a good relationship between the Moon and Mars. Mars, god of all things macho, symbolizes our energy or chi, our strength, entrepreneurial qualities, sexuality, ability to set boundaries, and immune system, as well as our military tendencies, temper, explosions, and accidents.

**If the Moon is in a supporting aspect to Mars**, we are lent strength, machismo, and protectiveness. These aspects can help us lift rocks or move a piano, spark passion, or help us to establish clear boundaries and clarify what we want and need. Our yes means yes and our no means no.

**If the Moon is in a challenging aspect to Mars**, irritability, willfulness, anger, and aggression may be evident, inspiring a belligerent, competitive, or contrary attitude–we can debate even simple household chores. We become more easily frustrated and can get distracted and therefore careless.

If you start feeling twitchy or raring for a fight, get physical. Exercise or chop wood, scrub a floor or take a brisk walk, and then come back and finesse that argument. If you suddenly feel accident-prone while cooking breakfast, acknowledge what you want or what upsets you,if only to yourself, and you'll feel safer carrying that cup of coffee and slicing a bagel.

## 2 The moon in relationship to ...

# Jupiter

Do you need a bigger perspective, to ask for a raise, run a charity ball, get the word out? Choose a sweet relationship between the Moon and Jupiter. Jupiter, the god who thought he ruled everything, symbolizes how we open up our world through education, law, philosophy, travel, abundance, expansive spirit, and seeing the bigger picture.

**If the Moon is in a supporting aspect to Jupiter**, it inspires generosity, abundance, optimism, and a philosophical ability to stand back and work for the good of the whole. We need space and freedom, a break, a whiff of far horizons. It's a good time to ask for a raise or encourage the generosity of others, to give hugs, to love and support ourselves. It's also a good time to publish, promote, or launch any project that needs visibility, goodwill, or a large audience.

**If the Moon is in a challenging aspect to Jupiter**, we can be led to overdo or overindulge, tempted to spend too much, give too much, promise too much, or overeat. These aspects encourage a tendency to do so much for someone else that we disempower that person and encourage bad behavior.

If you feel drawn to the challenging aspects of the Moon in Jupiter, take a moment to stand back and find a more philosophical or global perspective. What can your generous heart do to keep a balance and help all involved (yourself included) to feel healthy, satisfied, and empowered?

## ♄ The moon in relationship to … Saturn

Do you need to get organized, learn a skill, set a boundary, claim personal authority? Work with a good relationship between the Moon and Saturn. Saturn, seen as Father Time or Mother Crone, symbolizes boundaries, structure, mastery, traditions, bones, teeth, discipline, training, maturity, limitations, authority, policing, and prisons.

**If the Moon is in a supporting aspect to Saturn**, security and structure are the main features. These aspects help us tap into our adult self and learn from the teachers around us and the teacher within us. We can more easily organize our thoughts and our desk, tap into tradition, and buckle down to a task that takes concentration. It's a good time to deal with dentists, chiropractors, senior people, courts, and legal bureaucracies.

**If the Moon is in a challenging aspect to Saturn**, it can make us feel like the grown-up in the room–cranky, tired, authoritarian, stuck, old, creaky, stiff, brittle, humorless–which can then leave us depressed.

Take a moment to get organized and then tap into something you know well–do what you're good at doing and the depression eases. Realize that you are not stuck, although you may need to work a little longer. Stretch the body and stretch the mind to regain limberness.

## The moon in relationship to … Uranus

Do you need to try something new? Experiment with an interesting relationship between the Moon and Uranus. Uranus, god of primordial procreative chaos, is our cosmic clutch, helping us to change, to let go of an old gear and try a new one. Uranus speaks of change, electricity, excitement, genius, and anything that is erratic and chaotic.

**If the Moon is in a supporting aspect to Uranus**, we are inspired and ready for something completely different. A good Uranus–Moon aspect helps us to let go of what is safe and familiar and try something new. This helps when pitching a new proposal or experimenting with an art project. Take children on a field trip or work in a laboratory and engage inspiration and curiosity. Let go of an old love or toss out those shoes that are all worn out but hard to release. Move furniture around to try a new arrangement. Buy a high-tech product or download a new app. Experiment.

**If the Moon is in a challenging aspect to Uranus**, it can bring restlessness, anxiety, and irritability. We can make a change for change's sake, and not because it really is an improvement, or resist change because it makes us so uncomfortable. We tend to push away from the familiar, from the people we know and love just for a minute, and may find it easier to talk to strangers.

Take a break rather than quit. Walk down a road you've never walked down before. If you're in a meeting and becoming irritated with either your resistance to change, or theirs, just five minutes spent walking down the hall and back can help lower tension levels and help you to find a good way to bring a fresh approach, the positive use of Uranus, into the room.

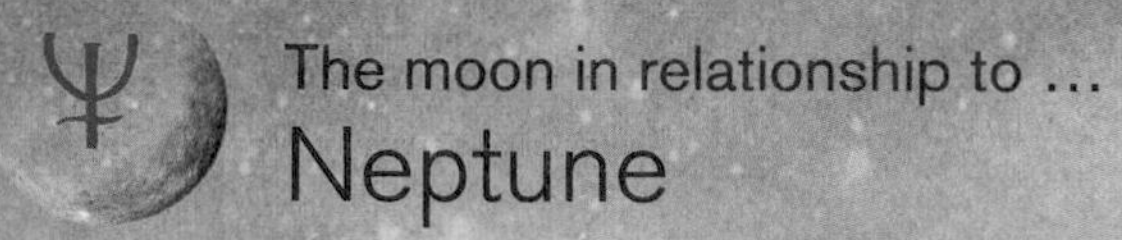

## The moon in relationship to ... Neptune

Do you need to be inspired, pray, meditate, intuit, dream an impossible dream? Choose a warm relationship between the Moon and Neptune. Neptune symbolizes spirituality, imagination, feeling at one with the whole, intuition, water, liquid, oil, illusion, delusion, escapism, alcoholism, addiction.

**If the Moon is in a supporting aspect to Neptune**, we are helped to tap into the dream world, growing more sensitive to our creative muse. We become more permeable, intuitive, and compassionate, connecting easily with our meditation and prayers. Our imagination is open and flowing, so it may be easier to share our dreams with others and brainstorm possibilities.

**If the Moon is in a challenging aspect to Neptune**, our escapist edges may be stirred, or we may feel out of sorts and confused. We can have trouble telling the difference between our hopes, fears, and intuition–they all blend together. Water or liquids can become problematic–a cup of tea may spill into the keyboard, for example. Alternatively, we may just feel sleepy.

You may notice that your mind just isn't on your work. You're feeling so sensitive that you drift and dream, imagining what would happen if you won the lottery. You're living in a fantasy instead of using your fantasy to enrich your life. That glass of wine sings to you, the fantasy novels and travel brochures beckon, or Morpheus calls you to take a nap. Give Neptune its due. Take a moment to rest and dream consciously. Meditate or pray for long enough to feel connected to spirit, or schedule some time out later in the day and promise yourself you'll get back to the dream as soon as this work is done.

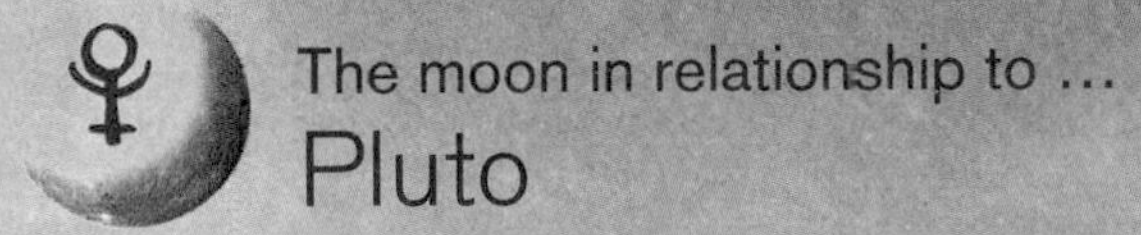

## The moon in relationship to … Pluto

Do you need to get to the bottom of something, a moment of solitude, to let go, to find the power within or a missing item? Look for a good relationship between the Moon and Pluto.

**If the Moon is in a supporting aspect to Pluto**, we can dive deep. It's a good aspect to do research, investigate, and search for what's missing. We often need a moment alone, a feeling that is more comfortable for introverts than it is for extroverts. A gentle ache can bring up memories of people, places, and things that we've released in the past, and remind us to be grateful. We can look within and find new resources, so it is a good aspect for psychotherapy or personal development, or to find the gumption to take on a challenge.

**If the Moon is in a challenging aspect to Pluto**, the door to our psychic basement opens, and we must choose how to respond. These aspects can take us in two directions. We may feel loss, loneliness, obsession, or a whiff of depression. If only for an hour or two, our minds can wiggle our soul's sore tooth. Alternatively, we may struggle with power, feel a tug-of-war of wills, or feel disempowered and bitter. Quite literally, we can run out of fuel or have sewage or garbage problems.

To counteract this, find something to concentrate on. Choose to sit with memories but give yourself a time limit—one hour to sit with old photos or love letters, say—and then move on. Write down memories that percolate to the surface. Listen to the soul's concerns, but don't get stuck there. Reconsider the concerns tomorrow. Take one small task and get to the bottom of it. Ask for a hug.

# Part IV
# Appendix

Discover the tools you need for moon wisdom. Gain a greater understanding of astrology, including how to read an astrological calendar and how to find your Moon sign, aspects, and phase.

# How to read an astrological calendar

Every astrological calendar has its quirks and comes with its own instruction, but usually the Moon sign of the day is shown in the top right-hand corner. When the Moon changes signs that day, expect two signs with the time of the change. In the lower left corner will be a list of relationships (aspects) the Moon forms with other planets. Each relationship grows in strength for hours ahead of time until it peaks at the time given, and then the Moon releases that planet and moves to the next aspect listed.

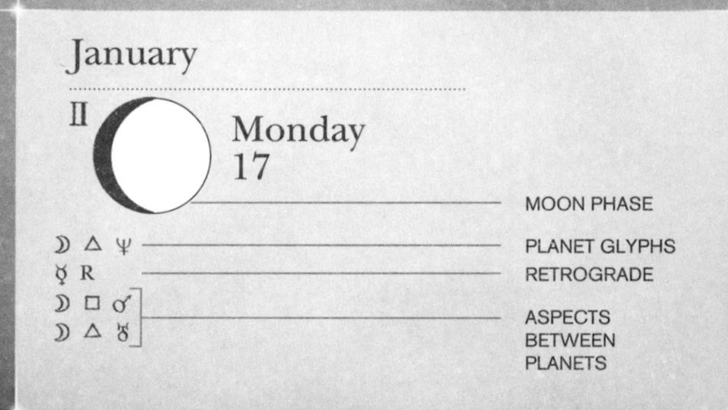

## Planet Symbols

|  |  |
| --- | --- |
| ☽ | Moon |
| ☉ | Sun |
| ☿ | Mercury |
| ♀ | Venus |
| ♂ | Mars |
| ♃ | Jupiter |
| ♄ | Saturn |
| ♅ | Uranus |
| ♆ | Neptune |
| ♇ | Pluto |
| ☊ | Node |
| Mc | Midheaven |
| As | Ascendant |

## Sign Symbols

|  |  |
| --- | --- |
| ♈ | Aries |
| ♉ | Taurus |
| ♊ | Gemini |
| ♋ | Cancer |
| ♌ | Leo |
| ♍ | Virgo |
| ♎ | Libra |
| ♏ | Scorpio |
| ♐ | Sagittarius |
| ♑ | Capricorn |
| ♒ | Aquarius |
| ♓ | Pisces |

## Aspect Symbols

|  |  |
| --- | --- |
| ☌ | Conjunction |
| ☍ | Opposition |
| △ | Trine |
| □ | Square |
| ⚹ | Sextile |
| ∠ | Semisquare |
| ⚺ | Semisextile |
| ⚻ | Quincunx |
| Q | Quintile |
| ⚼ | Sesquiquadrate |
| ⑦ | Septile |
| ⑨ | Novile |
| Bq | Biquintile |

# How to find your Moon sign, aspects, and phase

For the Moon sign and phase of the moment, you can purchase an astrological calendar or go online.

For a paper calendar, I recommend the following: WeMoon calendar (I write for them), Llewellyn's Astrological calendars, or Jim Maynard's Celestial influences. For online astrological information about the day or your own natal chart, I recommend my weekly blog, "Starcodes," on roanrobbins.com, as well as astro.com, zodiacarts.com, myastrology.net, cafeastrology.com, and astrologyclub.org.

For smartphones, search your app store for one on phases and aspects of the Moon.

The field is changing all the time. To get the most up-to-date sites, just do an internet search. The questions to use are:

- Astrologically, what phase is the Moon today?
- Astrologically, what aspects does the Moon make today?
- Natal astrological chart
- What phase was the Moon the day I was born?

# The keys of astrology

**The zodiac** The band of sky that the Sun appears to pass through on its yearly journey is divided into 12 signs or sections. Of course, the Sun is barely moving—our Earth rotates around the Sun—but from our position, we see the backdrop change and use that backdrop to describe the energetic quality we notice.

Several thousand years ago, on the first day of spring, that moment when the day and night are of equal length, the Sun was visible against a collection of stars that humans named Aries, the Ram. We didn't name it the ram because the stars painted so clear a picture of a male sheep (seriously, what do the stars know about a sheep?) Those stars have no real relationship to one another other than the pattern formed from our perspective here on Earth. We gave it the name because the energy of this time of year, the first month after the spring equinox, felt so brash and fresh, boisterous and pushy, like a ram.

Slowly, over the last few thousand years, the Sun itself traveled through the galaxy, and the spring equinox no longer occurs while the Sun is directly in front of this constellation. It has moved about a half-constellation forward. Western astrology, used in Europe and the Americas, follows the relationship of the Earth and Sun, and we have

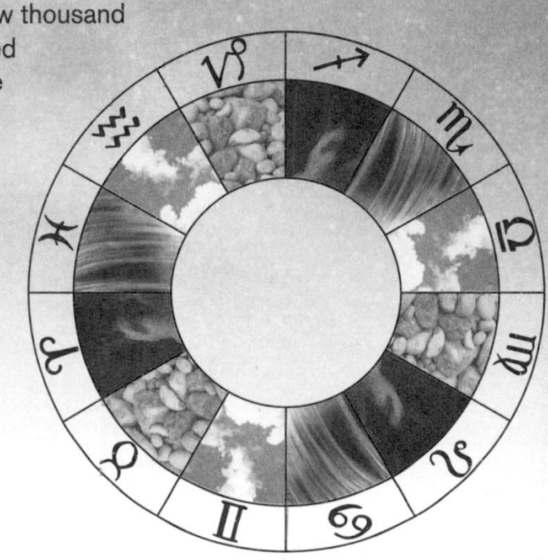

anchored the zodiac so that the spring equinox still begins the sign Aries, and the summer solstice begins Cancer.

Eastern or sidereal astrology, used mainly in India and Tibet, but which also has a following in the west, follows the stellar constellations themselves. Both systems use the same names for the signs, which can be very confusing. You could be a Libra in the west, but a Virgo in the sidereal system. Both systems work as long as the practitioners stay internally consistent within their chosen approach. Think of it like cutting an orange in different directions; each slice looks different but is from the same orange, neither is right or wrong, and together the images may give us the clearest picture possible.

**The horoscope** When an astrologer looks at your natal chart or horoscope, he/she looks at the pattern of the whole solar system when you were born as seen from the place of your birth. This is the blueprint that you get to express in your own way–free will and grace determine how you live out the pattern. It is a map of the psyche populated by the Sun, Moon, and planets, expressed through signs, and in the houses.

**The Sun and Moon** The light in the chart is provided by the Sun and Moon. The Sun, expressed through the sign of your birth, gives the qualities that act like the skeleton of personality upon which the remainder of the chart rests. The Moon is as important as the Sun and can underline the qualities of your Sun's sign, or add a counterpoint that can explain a lot. Say, for example, you're a supposedly quiet Virgo, but your Aries Moon blazes in impatient enthusiasm, or an outgoing Leo with a shy Cancer Moon, not sure whether you want to go to the party.

**The planets** Each one expresses a part of your personality. In global mythology, the characteristics of the planets are amazingly similar.

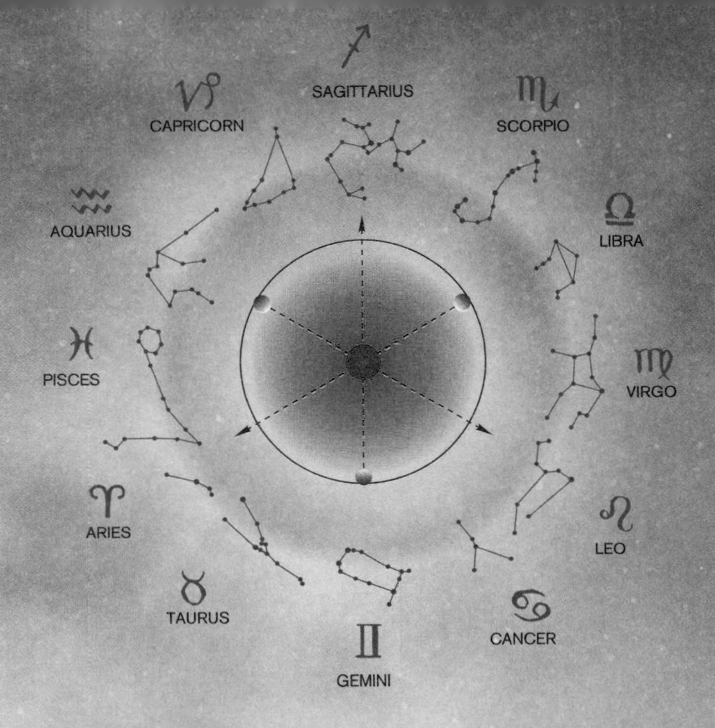


**Signs** Each planet is placed against the backdrop of a sign. We can think of them as being clothed in that sign, or as their light being expressed through that sign, like a red film over a stage light, which gives a warm glow. We work with geometry in astrology, so the circle of the zodiac is described in 360 degrees, and each sign takes up 30 degrees.

**Rising sign or ascendant** There are two ways of saying the same thing. If you could have stood up and pointed to the eastern horizon at the moment of your birth, the degree of the zodiac just ascending as the Earth turns would indicate your rising sign, the window through which you see the world and the world sees you. If you were born at the moment of sunrise, the Sun and rising sign would be one and the same.

**The houses** The ascendant is the doorway, or cusp, of the first house. The full horoscope is divided into 12 houses, which describe compartments or stage settings in our life—for example, personality, material resources, how we communicate, and home life. When we look at a chart, we can think of it like a game of Clue. Who did the crime? Colonel Mustard, with a candlestick, in the drawing room. Who instigated it? Mars, in Aries, in the first house. Our psyche is built over time, and the chart can also be read as the stages of life that formed us. The first house is related to our infancy, the 5th house to early romance, 7th to growing partnership, 10th to career peak, 12th to the introspection of old age.

**Aspects** The lines of communication between the planets form geometric patterns, which are called the aspects. Hard or challenging aspects, such as an opposition or a square (90 degrees apart), can act like a tough teacher whom you may not like but who dares you to step up to the plate and grow. The easier aspects, such as a trine (120 degrees), create connections, alliances between abilities. For example, if your Mercury, which rules the mind and communications ability, trines Uranus, a planet of ingenuity and invention, you tend to think fast and work well with inventive technology.

**Modalities** The nature of the signs is expressed as cardinal, fixed, or mutable. These are the modalities. Beside describing the signs, they act as shorthand for figuring aspects—signs in the same modality square or opposed one another.

**Cardinal** The signs are Aries, Cancer, Libra, and Capricorn. They come at the start of each season and are great for any beginnings, whereas follow-up is an acquired skill.

**Fixed signs** These are Taurus, Leo, Scorpio, and Aquarius. They come in the middle of each season, when the weather is steadier. Fixed signs are steady and stubborn.

**Mutable** Mutable signs are Gemini, Virgo, Sagittarius, and Pisces. They end each season, when the weather changes as one season mutates into another. Mutable signs adjust, explain, and mutate easily; they may have trouble initiating change.

Elements The basic vibe of the signs is expressed in elements. To understand the nature of the elements, take a walk and check out the quality of earth, air, fire, and water.

**Fire** signs are Aries, Leo, and Sagittarius. They are quick, passionate, extroverted, and enthusiastic.

**Earth** signs are Taurus, Virgo, and Capricorn. They are steady, pragmatic, sensual, fertile, and strong, with an introverted streak.

**Air** signs are Gemini, Libra, and Aquarius. They are outgoing, thought or ideal oriented, communicators, and networkers.

**Water** signs are Cancer, Scorpio, and Pisces. They are introspective, emotion-based, potentially nurturing, and sensitive.

# Resources

## Websites

To get a free copy of your chart, go to:
www.astro.com

My website with Starcodes weekly astrological weather forecast:
www.roanrobbins.com

www.astroinquiry.com
www.astrotheme.com
www.mountainastrologer.com
www.planetwatcher.com
www.skyscript.co.uk
www.stariq.com

## Podcast

Access Astrology on Blogtalk radio

## Organizations

The Astrological Lodge of London
www.astrolodge.co.uk

ISAR: The International Society for Astrological research
www.isarastrology.com

NCGR: National Council for Geocosmic Research
www.geocosmic.org

## Books

*The Inner Sky* by Steven Forrest

*Making the Gods Work for You: The Astrological Language of the Psyche* by Caroline Casey

*The Twelve Houses* by Howard Sasportas

*Introduction to Traditional Natal Astrology* by Charles Obert

Para Research's series on the planets:
*Planets in Houses* by Robert Pelletier
*Planets in Aspect* by Robert Pelletier
*Planets in Transit* by Rob Hand